Mediterranean Tomato Galette - page 86

Porridge Spelt Bread - page 94

Pumpkin and Cheese Crackers - page 122

Swedish Cinnamon Buns

Chocolate-Cherry Cheesecake - page 168

Muesli Bars - page 176

Pancakes - page 178

Artisan
SOURDOUGH
BREAD AND BEYOND

Care & Feeding of Your Sourdough Starter
Plus Recipes for European Breads, Pastas, Pancakes, Desserts, and More

Sonja Bauer
with Photography by Julia Hildebrand

© 2018, 2025, Christian Verlag GmbH, Munich, Germany
Author: Sonja Bauer
All rights reserved. *Artisan Sourdough: Bread and Beyond* is a revised and expanded second edition of the 2018 version originally published by Der Sauerteig under the title *Zeit für gute Brötchen* in Germany. This version published by Fox Chapel Publishing Company, Inc.

Team for Fox Chapel edition:

Editor: Madeline DeLuca

Proofread: Kurt Conley

Design: Freire. Serveis editorials, SL

To learn more about the other great books from Fox Chapel Publishing, or to find a retailer near you, call toll-free 800-457-9112 or visit us at www.FoxChapelPublishing.com.

We are always looking for talented authors.

To submit an idea, please send a brief inquiry to acquisitions@foxchapelpublishing.com.

Or write to:
Fox Chapel Publishing
903 Square Street
Mount Joy, PA 17552

Softcover ISBN: 978-1-4971-0570-6
Hardcover ISBN: 978-1-4971-0587-4

Library of Congress Control Number: 2025935387

Printed in China

Team for German edition:

Product management: Stefanie Gückstock

Editor: Constanze Lüdicke

Proofread: Franziska Sorgenfrei

Layout: Elke Mader

Cover design: Helen Garner

Reproduction: LUDWIG:media

Preparation: Julia Hegele

Printed in Türkiye by Elma Basim

Text and recipes: Sonja Bauer

Picture credits: Julia Hildebrand: Pages 11 (bottom), 35, 37, 39, 41, 43, 45, 47, 49, 51, 53, 55, 72, 77, 79, 81, 83, 85, 129, 153, 155, 157, 159, 163, 167, 171, 173, 175, 177, 179, 181, 183, 185, 187; Sonja Bauer: Pages 4, 5, 14, 18, 23, 28, 60, 61, 66, 67, 73, 90, 91, 96, 97, 102, 103, 108, 109, 114, 115, 121, 123, 125, 126, 134, 135, 139, 141, 143, 145, 148, 149, 165; Page 2, 190 top: Kerstin Hojka; Page 191 bottom: Ingolf Hatz; Page 189: Biomühle-Eiling.

FOREWORD

One of the best things about baking is that you are never too old to sharpen up your skills, so I was delighted to discover *Artisan Sourdough: Bread and Beyond*. These pages are full of all sorts of recipes for different sourdough loaves as well as intriguing ways to use up leftover sourdough, all thoroughly explained and beautifully illustrated. If you've never made sourdough before or, like me, are interested in learning different techniques and trying new recipes, Sonja's clear and precise descriptions of the processes involved make this book the perfect place to start. She guides you through the process of caring for your starter, replenishing it ready for next time, and shows you many ideas on what you can make with your bubbling creation.

About 20 years ago, while researching recipes for a book on pancakes, I made my first sourdough starter. It was a simple flour-and-water blend, which is used to make the half bread/half pancake Ethiopian specialty, injera. I was fascinated to see two simple ingredients, over three to four days, turn into a softly bubbling concoction that I could use to give this delicious bake its light, airy texture and slightly acidic flavor.

Bread has been enjoyed all over the world for centuries. Since humans began using tools, they were able to make basic dough from ground seeds and grains mixed with water that was cooked over fire as flatbreads. The ancient Egyptians are credited with leavening bread, although it probably started by accident when a traditional unleavened mix got contaminated with wild yeasts in the air and started to ferment. The attentive baker must have taken note of the resulting aerated mixture which was lighter in texture than the usual flat-baked loaves, and a new type of bread was born.

Immigrant settlers introduced their own ways of making bread to their adopted countries and began substituting familiar ingredients from their native cultures with those more readily available in their new surroundings. New flavors, textures, and presentations of bread became commonplace and from humble beginnings as an everyday staple. Bread developed in many shapes and forms throughout time. I associate Central Europe with archetypal sourdough baking. Specifically, rye bread from Germany with its crisp, floury crust and wiry, aerated crumb and tangy acidic taste; the bubbly, chewy dough of Italian ciabatta with its shattering crust; and the spongy crumb of French sourdough which uses a short-ferment "poolish" starter.

With our ever-growing concern for the quality of food we eat and the impact of intensive farming on the environment, choosing to make your own bread can help towards making a difference by careful selection of ingredients. Naturally fermented food is easier to digest and in turn, better for your gut. After several months of my giving up wheat and yeast due to ill health, a nutritionist suggested reintroducing a bread made from spelt flour and a natural rye and water starter. Not only did the bread taste very good after months of deprivation, but to my delight I found that eating it did not see a return of my digestive problems.

During the COVID-19 lockdown, when we had so much time on our hands, we turned to baking. With little effort, we were able to make a loaf from basic ingredients. Following a few simple rules, we coaxed our starters into life and nurtured and cared for them like babies. It was an easy-to-manage process, which gave us the perfect distraction from the uncontrollable pandemic in the world outside. The new sourdough generation of bakers have created lives and personalities for their bakes on social media. They share the ingredients they choose to use and offer technical and cooking tips. Some are even naming their starters. It's not something I've ever considered, but if I did, I would follow the very British form of naming anything that requires a moniker by calling it Doughy McDoughface.

As well as the creativity making bread can bring, there is something soothing about making a loaf. Kneading is good for relieving tension, and the length of time it takes to rise is an excellent test for patience. And let's not forget the rewards. Not only the deliciously tempting aromas during cooking, but there is also the unmatched taste and texture of freshly baked bread, and the satisfaction that you feel from your achievement.

It's quite likely that you're not going to get it right the first time and you may well end up in a sticky mess, but please don't be discouraged—it's all part of learning something new. Remember the old saying, "Practice makes perfect"? This really does apply to making bread. Once you've read Sonja's explanations and become familiar with the different stages and processes, the look and smell of the starter, and the feel of the dough, making sourdough and other types of bread will become second nature. You're about to embark on a culinary journey, and I'm sure this book will be your route map to success. Happy baking everyone!

Kathryn Hawkins
Author of *Complete Starter Guide to Making Bread, Self-Sufficiency: Breadmaking*, and more

66

114

TABLE OF CONTENTS

Foreword 3
Preface 7

SOURDOUGH: THE BASICS 9
Sourdough: The Basics, Science, and History 10
Establishing a Starter 13
Sourdough Starter Care 16
Tips for Working with Sourdough 18
Rye Sourdough 20
Wheat Sourdough 22
Lievito Madre 25
Preserving Sourdough 27
Side Note on Bread Baking 30
Guide to the Recipes 32
Essential Tools for Sourdough Baking 33

SIDE DISHES 35
Naan Bread 36
Wheat Tortillas 38
Potato Gnocchi 40
Spätzle 42
Fresh Pasta 44
Spelt Pasta 46
Herb Crêpes 48

Semmelknödel (Bread Dumplings) 50
Palatinate-Style Steamed Dumplings 52
Quick Sourdough Waffles 54
Hobak Buchimgae with Sesame Dip Sauce 56

PIZZA, QUICHE & CO. 59
Focaccia 60
Pinsa Romana 64
Italian Pizza 66
Crispy Pan Pizza 70
Kiymali Pide 72
Alsatian-Style Beer Cream Flatbread 76
Tarte Flambée 78
Onion Tart 80
Salmon-Spinach Tart 82
Quiche Lorraine 84
Mediterranean Tomato Galette 86

BREAD & ROLLS 89
Refreshing Bread for Sourdough Leftovers 90
Porridge Spelt Bread 94
Rustic Beer Crust 96
Country Loaf 100
Wholemeal Rye and Spelt Bread 102

4 ARTISAN SOURDOUGH: BREAD AND BEYOND

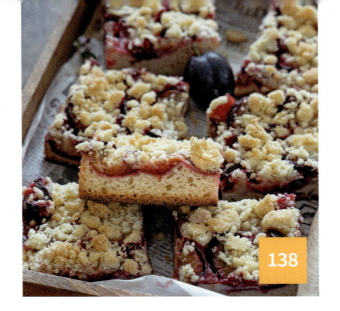

Smoky Almond and Bacon Twisted Rolls. 106	Torta di Nocciole 162
Olive Oil Brioche Burger Buns 108	Torta di Mandorle 164
Wheat Rolls 112	Brookies 166
Spelt and Oat Rolls 114	Chocolate-Cherry Cheesecake with Crumble 168

NIBBLES 119

Breadsticks with Parmesan Crust. 120
Pumpkin and Cheese Crackers 122
Taralli Pugliesi 124
Grissini. 126
Crispy Crackers 128
Asian-Style Crackers 130

SWEETS FOR BREAKFAST & DESSERT . . .171

Granola 172
Overnight Baked Oatmeal 174
Muesli Bars 176
Pancakes 178
Grandma's Apple Pancakes 180
Dutch Baby 182
Caramelized Kaiserschmarren 184
Baked Bananas with Honey 186
Liége Waffles 188

SWEET BAKED GOODS 133

Swedish Cinnamon Rolls. 134
Plum Cake with Crumble 138
Blueberry Quark Cookies. 140
Sourdough Babka 144
Yeast Braid with Milk Sourdough 148
Buchteln (Sweet Rolls) 152
Fermented Apple Pie 154
Banana Bread 156
Raspberry White Chocolate Muffins 158
Fudgy Brownies 160

About the Author 190
About the Photographer 190
Sourdough Index 191
Index 191

PREFACE

Sourdough is primarily known in the world of bread baking and, for many passionate home bakers, it is the stuff dreams are made of: the heart of numerous good, wholesome, and flavorful breads. In the beginning, it is often both a challenge and a motivation to improve and develop one's own "skills." Baking with sourdough has a certain magic and fascination, yet at the same time, it quickly brings you back down to earth when things don't go as planned. Fermentation is an art.

A "good sourdough" needs to be nurtured and cared for. Some people even maintain several different types. In the process, leftovers often accumulate—too precious to simply discard. So-called "refresher recipes" for bread and rolls with leftover sourdough are therefore very popular.

This book offers numerous recipes to make use of excess sourdough. But beyond that, it also contains many other exciting recipes featuring sourdough. Always true to the motto: Sourdough is so much more. It can enrich (almost) anything in the kitchen. From pancakes to onion tarts, the possibilities are endless, and the best is: dishes refined with sourdough are always especially delicious and aromatic!

That's why this book provides a comprehensive introduction to sourdough—covering the essential basics and a diverse collection of recipes for every taste, reimagined classics, and certainly some new favorite recipes!

Wishing you lots of joy in fermenting, creative cooking, and baking with sourdough.

Yours,

Sonja Bauer

Author, nutritional expert, and founder of Cookie and Co. food blog

SOURDOUGH: THE BASICS, SCIENCE, AND HISTORY

SOURDOUGH: THE BASICS, SCIENCE, AND HISTORY

Sourdough is trending. Baking with sourdough has made a big comeback recently. But sourdough is not just a fad; rather, it's one of the oldest methods for making baked goods more digestible. Sourdough was discovered by chance thousands of years ago and was used by the ancient Egyptians and Greeks. Today, we still use this method by letting the dough ferment.

The fermentation of doughs is based on a natural fermentation process by lactic acid bacteria and wild yeasts, which are naturally present in the flour. During fermentation, they metabolize the flour components and produce carbon dioxide (CO_2), which ultimately leads to the dough's rising. At the same time, complex flavors are created, and the digestibility and shelf life of the baked goods are improved.

WHAT IS SOURDOUGH?

Sourdough is a natural leavening agent and a mixture of water, flour, natural yeast, and a microflora of microorganisms. In every active sourdough, billions of lactic acid bacteria and millions of yeast cells live. Without these microorganisms, there would be no sourdough, as they provide the flavor and the leavening power, making the baked goods tasty and airy. Sourdough baked goods always contain yeast, even if no commercial yeast is added.

There are many different types of sourdough. The flavor and leavening power of sourdough depend heavily on the activity and composition of the microorganisms. Each sourdough is unique, and so are the baked goods made with it.

In Germany and Austria, rye sourdough is common, while in France, Italy, and globally, wheat sourdough is mostly used. In America, white flour is often used for sourdough. Different countries have their own recipe references and traditions for making sourdough. Whether it's rye, wheat, or white sourdough, all are made from dough with living microorganisms. This dough ferments for several days and, with regular care, stays alive and active.

SOURDOUGH THEN AND NOW

For a long time, sourdough was the only leavening agent. While in the past it was a cost-effective way to make bread dough rise, today, the focus is more on taste and nutritional benefits.

Sourdough was of particular importance when baking with rye flour. In addition to its function as a leavening agent, sourdough made rye flour suitable for baking in the first place. This was due to the enzyme-inhibiting effect of the lactic and acetic acids produced by the lactic acid bacteria. For this reason, there are still recommendations in the home baking community to add lemon juice or vinegar to bread doughs to replace the missing sourdough. However, modern rye varieties now contain much lower enzyme levels than in the past, making the use of sourdough no longer strictly necessary.

With industrialization, many ready-made sourdough products appeared on the market. For home use, you can find pasteurized, liquid "natural sourdough" in plastic bags at supermarkets and dried sourdough powder, called "sourdough extracts," in drugstores. However, these products have no leavening power and are intended solely as flavor enhancers. The complex flavors created during the fermentation of doughs can't be replaced or replicated by these products.

For the recipes in this book, only active sourdough is used.

Today, particularly in online shops, active sourdough starters are also available in the form of fresh sourdough starter or in powdered form. These are established sourdough starters that can either be further maintained or used to easily start a sourdough starter. However, it is crucial to ensure that the starters are active sourdough starters when purchasing, and not just flavor enhancers. Additionally, there are online platforms where sourdough starters are exchanged or sold (like www.culturesforhealth.com).

WHAT IS FERMENTATION?

Fermentation (also known as "leavening") using lactic acid bacteria and yeasts is one of the oldest processes for improving the digestibility and preservation of food. Not only bread, but also beer, wine, vinegar, yogurt, cheese, chocolate, vanilla beans, and olives are transformed into what they are through fermentation. One of the most well-known examples is sauerkraut.

When flour and water are mixed for sourdough and left to sit for a long period of time, the microorganisms naturally present in the flour, originating from the grain's husk, begin to multiply. Under favorable conditions and with sufficient food for the microorganisms, a stable microflora of the desired microorganisms gradually establishes itself, forming a natural protection against spoilage and mold growth.

During fermentation, complex processes take place. Simply put, enzymes in sourdough break down the starches and sugars in the flour into glucose, which feeds the microorganisms. Homofermentatic lactic acid bacteria mainly produce lactic acid from glucose, while heterofermentative lactic acid bacteria also create alcohol, acetic acid, and carbon dioxide. Yeasts produce carbon dioxide and, in the absence of oxygen, alcohol.

These metabolic by-products lead to the loosening of the dough, while simultaneously, complex and intense flavor compounds are formed. However, fermentation does not always have to be successful. Sometimes, the "wrong" microorganisms, such as spoilage bacteria, can take over and should not be cooked with.

Microorganisms, including wild yeasts and lactic acid bacteria, are present on the surface of grain kernels and are transferred into the flour during the milling process. The more outer layers a flour contains, the more microorganisms it has. Using flour from organic farming gives a clear advantage when making sourdough, as the number of microorganisms on the surface of the grain is greatly reduced in conventional grain farming due to pesticide use.

IS SOURDOUGH HEALTHY?

Although baked goods made with sourdough are generally made from the same raw ingredients as other baked goods, the long fermentation process improves their nutritional properties. Sourdough makes baked goods overall more digestible and promotes their digestibility, as the microorganisms break down or at least split hard-to-digest components in the grain products. In a way, a kind of "pre-digestion" occurs.

One example of this is certain sugar molecules that, due to their structure, are poorly broken down in the small intestine and thus pass undigested into the large intestine, where they are decomposed by bacteria, leading to digestive discomfort.

Additionally, certain proteins in gluten-containing grains are partially broken down, which in some people can trigger intestinal issues and are then mistakenly interpreted as wheat intolerance or true gluten intolerance (celiac disease).

Furthermore, sourdough improves nutrient absorption. Wholemeal flours and oat flakes in particular contain a lot of phytic acid or phytate. A substance that is useful for plants, but which leads to poorer absorption of minerals and trace elements such as calcium, potassium, iron, magnesium, and zinc in humans. The lactic acid bacteria from the sourdough lower the pH level in the dough during fermentation, which promotes the breakdown of phytates and thus increases mineral absorption in the body.

Scientists are also researching the extent to which the consumption of sourdough (bread) has a positive effect on the human intestinal microbiome and the beneficial effects on blood sugar and insulin levels.

CREATIVE COOKING WITH SOURDOUGH

Sourdough can enrich cooking and baking in many ways, not only with fantastic flavors but also with new and exciting approaches. In cooking, sourdough can also lead to better digestibility when part or even the entire flour content in foods has been fermented in sourdough beforehand. And it's a great way to use up sourdough starter and discard leftovers!

BAKING CAKES WITH SOURDOUGH

Are cakes with sourdough healthier? Of course, a cake is not automatically healthy just because it contains sourdough. Cakes, brownies, cookies, or yeast breads made with sourdough, which already contain fermented flour, are certainly not necessarily healthier, but they may be a little better tolerated and definitely more flavorful. After all, food must also be enjoyable and fun, and it's the variety and balance in the whole that matters! In addition, the psyche also plays a major role in health and a delicious piece of cake sometimes just makes you happy!

Fudgy Brownies (page 160).

Palatinate-Style Steamed Dumplings (page 52).

ESTABLISHING A STARTER

Sourdough baking requires using an active starter. This section will describe some methods to establish your starter and describe the care required to keep it strong. To put it bluntly, sourdough cultivation through spontaneous fermentation means that flour and water are mixed and then the dough takes time to form on its own. Essentially, it is a competition between the desired microorganisms (lactic acid bacteria and wild yeasts) and the unwanted microorganisms (mold and spoilage bacteria), which determines which ones gain the upper hand. With favorable conditions, the development of the desired microorganisms and the formation of a sourdough starter culture can be supported.

GENERAL TIPS & ADVICE

Once flour and water are mixed and left to sit for some time, the microorganisms begin to multiply and your starter begins to rise. **Sufficient warmth is important for sourdough cultivation** because the desired microorganisms multiply best under these conditions. A temperature range of 75–90°F (25–30°C) is considered ideal for sourdough cultivation. At cooler temperatures, this process typically proceeds very slowly or not at all, and it may result in excessive acidity.

The jar for the sourdough should have about three times the volume of the sourdough starter and a rather slim shape. Preserving jars are well

Alsatian-Style Beer Cream Flatbread (page 76).

Sourdough Babka (page 144).

ESTABLISHING A STARTER | 13

suited. These should be rinsed with hot water beforehand to remove any potential soap residues. Mark the filling level (for example, with a rubber band) to be able to assess the volume increase.

The leftover sourdough starter in the first few days should definitely be discarded. At the beginning, undesirable germs can also multiply. The young sourdough starter often has an unpleasant smell for this reason. Over time, the right microorganisms take over, and a stable microflora forms, which, in combination with the developing acidity, protects against unwanted germs. A newly cultivated sourdough culture will become stronger and more flavorful with regular care.

With this method, different types of sourdough starters can be made in parallel according to your preference.

ORGANIC WHOLEMEAL STARTER
Step 1: Sourdough starter
> 60 g water (104°F [40°C])
> 50 g organic wholemeal flour (e.g. spelt, rye or wheat)

Mix the water and flour thoroughly in a clean glass (with lid). Close the lid loosely. Place the mixture in a warm place at 75–90°F (25–30°C) for a total of 24 hours, stirring with a clean spoon after 12 hours.

Step 2: Feeding
> 50 g of the 1st sourdough starter
> 60 g water (104°F [40°C])
> 50 g organic wholemeal flour (e.g. spelt, rye or wheat)

Thoroughly mix the 50 g from the 1st sourdough starter with the warm water and the wholemeal flour in a clean jar (with a lid).

Close the lid loosely and place the mixture in a warm place at 75–90°F (25–30°C) for a total of 24 hours, stirring with a clean spoon after 12 hours.

From day 3 (2nd feeding) you can decide which sourdough you want to make and select your flour accordingly. You can now switch to a type of flour (for example Type-1150 rye flour or Type-1050 wheat or rye flour).

CULTIVATING RYE, WHEAT, OR SPELT SOURDOUGH
Step 3: 2nd–10th feeding
> 50 g of the last sourdough starter
> 50 g of water (104°F [40°C])
> 50 g flour (for example Type-1150 rye flour or Type-1050 wheat or rye flour)

Thoroughly mix the 50 g of the previous sourdough starter with the warm water and the flour in a clean jar. Transfer to a fresh clean jar (with a lid), loosely close the lid, and place the mixture in a 75–90°F (25–30°C) warm location for about 12 hours.

Repeat this process every 12 hours, unless the sourdough starter doubles in size faster. If that is the case, feed it earlier, always after the sourdough starter has at least doubled in size.

The time interval will gradually shorten.

By the fifth day, the sourdough starter should double in size within 12 hours. If that is not the case, continue with the same procedure until doubling takes place within this time frame.

CULTIVATING LIEVITO MADRE
Step 3: Feeding
> 50 g of the last sourdough starter
> 10 g water (104°F [40°C])
> 50 g flour (for example, Type-1050 or Type-550 wheat flour)

Thoroughly mix the 50 g of the previous sourdough starter with the water and flour. Transfer to a fresh clean jar (with a lid), loosely close the lid, and place the mixture in a 75–90°F (25–30°C) warm location for about 12 hours.

Step 4: 3rd-10th Feeding
> 50 g of the last sourdough starter
> 20–25 g water (104°F [40°C])
> 50 g of flour (for example, Type-1050 or Type-550 wheat flour)

Thoroughly mix the 50 g of the previous sourdough starter with the water and flour (the consistency should resemble marzipan). Transfer to a fresh clean jar (with a lid), loosely close the lid, and place the mixture in a 75–90°F (25–30°C) warm location for about 12 hours.

Repeat this process every 12 hours, unless the sourdough starter doubles in size faster. If that is the case, feed it earlier, always after the sourdough starter has at least doubled in size.

The time interval will gradually shorten. Within 7–10 days, the starter should double in size after 3–4 hours. If that is not the case, continue with the same procedure until doubling takes place within this time frame. The process may take a few extra days under less-than-ideal conditions.

For practical reasons, the Lievito Madre starter can be briefly stored in the fridge after it has doubled, for example overnight. Then, take the cold batch out of the fridge **1 hour** before the next feeding. **The finished Lievito Madre should have a mild sour or pleasantly fruity–fermented scent.**

Cultivated sourdoughs: Lievito Madre, wheat sourdough, rye sourdough (from left to right).

SOURDOUGH STARTER CARE

Every sourdough starter needs to be regularly cared for to remain active and alive. The microorganisms need fresh food.

The microbiota of sourdough is primarily influenced by the microorganisms and enzymes present in the flour. Characteristics such as flavor and leavening power can be specifically controlled by factors such as the type of flour used for feeding, the water content, temperature, ripening time, and the amount and quality of the starter in relation to the flour and water, as well as the frequency of feeding.

WHAT IS A STARTER?

The starter is a part of the sourdough that is stored in a closed container in the refrigerator so that it can be used to make new sourdough at a later date. Traditionally, a portion of the sourdough that was prepared for baking is set aside and stored until the next baking session to "seed" a new batch of sourdough. However, it is recommended to keep the starter separately so that the entire starter is not accidentally used.

When feeding, essentially a new sourdough is made each time from the stored starter, flour, and water. It is advisable to stick to the same type of flour as much as possible and not to switch constantly.

GOOD TO KNOW

If the wrong flour was used once for feeding, it is usually not a big issue; it takes a few feeding cycles for the culture to adjust. The next time, just continue feeding it with the usual flour.

HOW OFTEN SHOULD YOU FEED?

Regular care of the starter is essential. Keeping the parameters consistent allows specific characteristics of the sourdough to be controlled, such as a mild flavor.

To maintain sufficient activity, the starter should be fed **once a week**. Afterwards, it is stored in the refrigerator. For a mild, highly active, and strong starter, feeding it **twice a week** is recommended. If a starter is fed only for maintenance—not for baking—it should be placed in the refrigerator as soon as it has nearly doubled, or at the latest when it has fully doubled. This ensures that the microorganisms still have enough nutrients to sustain them for a while in the fridge.

IRREGULAR FEEDING

If the starter is fed much less frequently or inconsistently, a noticeable decrease in sourdough activity can be expected. This is especially relevant when baking without additional yeast. A gap of 10–14 days is usually not a problem for the sourdough, but 1 or 2 extra feeding cycles may be necessary before baking. If longer intervals between feedings are anticipated, it is advisable to refresh the starter with a firmer consistency to slow down the microorganisms' metabolism, ensuring that the nutrients last longer (see Preserving Sourdough page 27).

THE SOURDOUGH IS HUNGRY

If the starter smells like acetone (similar to nail polish remover), it is a clear sign that the nutrients have been largely depleted and the starter needs to be refreshed. If a starter goes too long without being refreshed, liquid will begin to separate on the surface—this is called "hooch." Initially, hooch is clear, but over time, it darkens. Hooch contains acids and alcohol, which provide a natural protection against mold growth. Some people prefer to keep the hooch in, since it adds flavor to the sourdough. If you do not want this, you can pour off the hooch before the next feeding.

KEY FACTORS FOR SOURDOUGH MANAGEMENT
There are many different ways to maintain a sourdough starter. The **quality of the starter**, **temperature**, **feeding frequency**, and **composition** (the **ratio of starter** and **water to flour**) all influence the character of the sourdough. These factors can be adjusted to create a mild, robustly aromatic, or even a tangy, sour flavor.

Feeding a starter for maintenance and preparing sourdough for baking can generally follow the same process.

Quality of the starter
If a starter is maintained in a warm environment with a mild profile, the resulting sourdough will also be milder. Conversely, a starter that is already sour will produce a more acidic sourdough. The key to strong leavening power in sourdough is primarily the activity of the starter. Frequent and consistent feedings increase activity, whereas irregular feedings make the starter sluggish.

Amount of starter
The higher the proportion of starter relative to flour and water in a sourdough, the faster it matures. In most cases, a sourdough with a high starter content will be quite mild because the fermentation time is relatively short.

Amount of water
The water used should be about 100°F (40°C) to ensure the sourdough starts at an optimal fermentation temperature. The more water a sourdough contains, the faster it ferments.

Flour
Each grain type carries its own unique microflora. However, not only the grain variety but also the degree of milling has a significant impact on the sourdough's characteristics. Light flours, i.e. flours with low type numbers, ferment rather mildly, whereas dark flours with higher type numbers (especially wholemeal flours) promote a stronger acidity and a stronger aroma.

The coarser the flour is ground—up to cracked grain—the longer fermentation will take.

The darker the flour used, the better the microorganisms are supplied with nutrients. Darker flours acidify more quickly, and their microflora stabilize faster, which is why sourdough is often cultivated with whole grain or darker flours.

Temperature
Temperature is a crucial factor in sourdough fermentation. Ensuring a sufficiently warm temperature at the beginning of fermentation is particularly important. Warmer temperatures slow the growth of acetic acid-producing microorganisms while favoring more yeast-friendly and lactic acid-producing microorganisms. Warm temperatures between 75–90°F (25–30°C) lead to mildly acidic flavors, while cooler temperatures between 68–75°F (20–24°C) result in a more pronounced sourness.

How can sufficient warmth be ensured?
In home environments, low room temperatures can pose a challenge for sourdough refreshing. Special

proofing machines are available for hobby bakers. However, there are many other and "cheaper" ways to achieve the right temperature for the sourdough. There are often some warmer places in the home that are suitable (always check the temperature with a room thermometer or infrared thermometer): Heating mat (for terrariums or plant cultivation) with thermostat in an insulated box; on the heater with a wooden board underneath (no direct contact); in the oven or in the microwave with the lamp switched on (unless this is an LED light); place a hot water bottle or PET bottle filled with hot water in the switched-off oven or in an insulated box or cool bag; on the underfloor heating or on the Internet router.

RULE OF THUMB

> The more starter used relative to flour, the faster and milder the sourdough ferments, and vice versa. In a warm environment, sourdough ferments significantly faster and milder than in a cooler one.

TIPS FOR WORKING WITH SOURDOUGH

REPLACE STARTER

It is generally better to maintain one well-kept, active starter in the refrigerator rather than several different ones that are only moderately maintained. Keeping multiple types of starter is only worthwhile if they are used regularly.

Alternatively, the starter used for sourdough preparation can be swapped. For example, Lievito Madre or liquid wheat starter can be used to ferment rye flour in a sourdough. In this case, the sourdough will tend to ferment very mildly. If only 10 g of starter is needed, Lievito Madre can be substituted for rye starter without issue—the firmer consistency of Lievito Madre won't affect such a small amount. If a larger quantity of starter is used, the water content in the recipe should be adjusted accordingly.

The reverse substitution is usually not ideal. For instance, if a strong rye starter is used instead of a mild wheat starter, the resulting flavors may be much more acidic than intended for the recipe. This is especially relevant for sweet recipes or doughs that undergo long, cold fermentation.

ADDITIONAL YEAST

Yeast is often a topic of debate when it comes to adding it to sourdough recipes.

Ultimately, this is a purely personal decision and a matter of taste. There is no right and no wrong. The best thing is to find your own way. As you gain experience, you can reduce or even omit the yeast in recipes.

Advantages

Adding a small amount of yeast to sourdough can have benefits. For example, it makes the fermentation process more predictable, requires less experience with sourdough maintenance, and can help when working with very young, recently cultivated sourdough cultures that are not yet fully developed in their leavening power.

Additionally, yeast can slow down the acidification of dough caused by sourdough, especially in long or cold fermentations.

For some baked goods, a subtle yeast flavor is actually desirable, particularly in sweet pastries or rolls. Adding yeast can also contribute to a softer, fluffier crumb.

Disadvantages

Yeast causes baked goods to stale more quickly—it accelerates the process of drying out. In contrast, pure sourdough bread has a significantly longer shelf life. Pure sourdough breads in particular have an incomparably aromatic taste. Often, it even gets better from day to day and it is exciting to taste this change.

Above a certain amount of yeast, an unpleasant yeast taste can occur (but this is subjective). In addition, doughs mature much faster, which can have additional disadvantages in terms of taste, digestibility, and freshness.

GENERAL GUIDELINES

If sourdough is the only leavening agent (without added yeast in the final dough), it needs to be very active and recently fed. Your best baking success is achieved when the sourdough is at peak rise.

If a sourdough starter takes significantly longer to rise than the time specified in recipes, this may indicate low activity or insufficient leavening power. Performing multiple consecutive feedings can help restore its strength. Feeding the sourdough with a slightly darker, more nutrient-rich flour can also help reinvigorate it.

Rye starter.

Wheat starter.

RYE SOURDOUGH

In German-speaking regions in Europe, when people refer to sourdough, they typically mean rye sourdough—the traditional sourdough used for popular breads such as mixed rye bread, pure rye bread, or black bread. The recipes in this book are designed for a mild rye starter.

In addition to bread making, rye sourdough or rye starter can also enrich creative cuisine as an unusual ingredient. Its bold flavors work particularly well in sweet baked goods that contain chocolate or cocoa, providing a rich and harmonious complexity, as you will discover when trying the recipes in this book.

KEY FACTS

Rye sourdough has intense flavors that give rye and rye-mixed breads their characteristic taste. Without it, these breads would be quite bland.

Additionally, sourdough makes rye bread more digestible. For example, for 100 g of rye flour you need 100 g of water. That is why it is often referred to as soft or liquid sourdough.

The classic **flour for maintaining rye starters** is Type-1150 rye flour (known as Type R 960 in Austria). However, other flour grades, such as Type-1370 or whole grain rye flour, can also be used. Additionally, coarsely milled rye (rye meal) can be fermented instead of flour.

Rye sourdough naturally produces more acidity compared to wheat or spelt sourdough, especially when maintained with whole grain rye flour over time.

A long cold dough fermentation is rather unusual with rye sourdough due to the more pronounced sour flavors. There may be noticeable acetic acid notes.

Rye sourdough cultures that are refreshed at room temperature (below 72 °F [22 °C]) over long periods often lack sufficient sourdough yeasts, which are crucial for leavening. To put it simply: the dough may not rise well.

When preparing **rye sourdough for baking**, it should at least double in volume before being incorporated into the dough. The surface should still have a slight dome shape and should not have collapsed yet.

When **refreshing the starter for maintenance**, it should be placed in the refrigerator as soon as it has doubled in volume—preferably even slightly earlier.

Unique and complex flavors can be created by using alternative liquids instead of water, such as coffee or non-alcoholic beer (since alcohol would inhibit microbial activity).

It is also possible to ferment different flour types together in one sourdough, creating what is known as a **mixed sourdough**—such as a blend of rye and wheat flour. A mixed sourdough is typically mild yet aromatic and strong in fermentation, even when using a one-step method. Both rye and wheat starter can be used. However, the mixed sourdough is usually much more aromatic with rye starter.

(You can find a recipe with mixed sourdough on page 104, Smoky Almond and Bacon Twisted Rolls.)

COMMON SOURDOUGH METHODS

The mildest method for regular refreshing is the **1:1:1 method**. This is also well-suited for baking. In this method, 1 part rye starter + 1 part warm water + 1 part rye flour are mixed and fermented at a warm temperature of 79–82 °F (26–28 °C). The mixture should double in volume within 2-4 hours.

Example 1:1:1
> 50 g rye starter
> 50 g warm water (104°F [40°C])
> 50 g Type-1150 rye flour

Thoroughly mix everything in a clean jar (with a lid), close the lid loosely, and allow the mixture to ferment at a warm place between 79–82°F (26–28°C) for about 2–4 hours.

A frequently used, very traditional method is the **single-stage sourdough fermentation**. The fermentation time is slightly longer, resulting in more intense flavors, but also more acidity. The single-stage sourdough is usually prepared at a ratio of 1:10:10. In this method, mix 1 part rye starter + 10 parts warm water + 10 parts rye flour and leave to ferment at room temperature for 10–12 hours. If the sourdough culture is very active, fermentation can proceed significantly faster. For better time management, the amount of starter can be halved, for example, when fermenting overnight.

Example of one-stage sourdough
> 10 g rye starter
> 100 g warm water (104°F [40°C])
> 100 g Type-1150 rye flour

Thoroughly mix everything in a clean jar (with a lid), close the lid loosely, and let the mixture ferment at room temperature (72°F [22°C]) for about 10–12 hours.

Rye sourdough is often made in several stages. **Two and three-stage fermentations** can create very aromatic and active sourdoughs by combining different fermentation phases. This book applies a two-stage sourdough fermentation, combining the previously described single-stage sourdough with the 1:1:1 method.

Also worth mentioning is salted sourdough, known as the **Monheimer Salzsauer process**, a single-stage rye sourdough fermentation with added salt. To compensate, the amount of starter is usually increased. Salt reduces acid formation in the sourdough, as it inhibits the activity of acid-producing microorganisms. As a result, fermentation slows down, and the maturation time extends. Breads made with salted sourdough generally have a balanced, mild aroma, similar to a multi-stage fermented sourdough.

CONVERTING RYE SOURDOUGH TO WHEAT SOURDOUGH

Rye sourdough → Liquid wheat sourdough
> 10 g rye starter
> 50 g warm water (104°F [40°C])
> 50 g Type-550 wheat flour

Thoroughly mix everything in a clean jar (with a lid) and close the lid loosely. Let the mixture ferment in a warm place 79–86°F (26–30°C) until it has doubled in volume

Then continue refreshing it as a wheat sourdough (see page 21). At least five refresh cycles are necessary to fully transition the sourdough culture.

Rye sourdough → Lievito Madre
> 10 g rye starter
> 20–25 g warm water (104°F [40°C])
> 50 g Type-550 wheat flour

Dissolve the rye starter in water, then knead it thoroughly with the flour. Place in a clean jar (with lid), close the lid loosely, and leave to mature in a warm place at 79–86°F (26–30°C) until it has doubled in volume.

Then continue refreshing it as a Lievito Madre (see page 24). At least five refresh cycles are needed to fully transition the sourdough culture.

WHEAT SOURDOUGH

Globally, wheat sourdough is the most widespread type. When people refer to *Levain liquide* in France, sourdough or Levain in English-speaking regions, or Li.co.li (*Lievito in coltura liquida*) in Italy, they mean liquid wheat sourdough. Wheat sourdough is the traditional leaven for popular French bread classics such as Tourte de Meule, Pain de Champagne, or Pain au Levain. It is also commonly used for baguettes, rolls, and even sweet baked goods. One of the most famous examples of wheat sourdough bread is San Francisco Sourdough Bread.

Beyond bread making, wheat sourdough or wheat starter can enrich creative cuisine as an aromatic ingredient. Both sweet and savory dishes benefit from its mild and complex flavors.

KEY FACTS

Wheat sourdough has a mild and aromatic flavor, making it particularly suitable for light baked goods such as rolls and white bread.

Liquid wheat sourdough typically consists of equal parts flour and water. For example, 100 g of wheat flour is mixed with 100 g of water. That is why it is often referred to as soft or liquid sourdough. Compared to rye sourdough, wheat sourdough is naturally softer and more fluid due to the properties of the flour. Sometimes, wheat sourdough is maintained at a slightly firmer consistency by using only 80 g of water per 100 g of wheat flour.

The classic flour for refreshing wheat starter is Type-550 wheat flour (in Austria, W 700). Type-1050 wheat flour is also well suited. Whole wheat flour can be used as well, but over time, it tends to produce more acidic flavors.

Particularly complex and almost floral aromas can develop in wheat sourdough when it is maintained with French wheat flours such as T 65 or T 80. It is important to ensure that these flours are free of additives such as ascorbic acid (vitamin C) or enzyme supplements, as these can interfere with fermentation.

A mild wheat sourdough is very well suited for a long cold dough preparation and can lead to highly aromatic baked goods, especially when prepared without yeast.

Although wheat sourdough cultures can theoretically be refreshed indefinitely at room temperature, they often lack sufficient sourdough yeasts over time, which are essential for dough leavening. This can lead to increasingly sour notes.

It is recommended to maintain a warm and mild fermentation process, both for refreshing and baking.

When preparing **wheat sourdough for baking**, it should at least double in volume before being mixed into the dough. Fully matured wheat sourdough should be filled with air bubbles and should not have started to collapse.

When refreshing the starter for maintenance, it should be placed in the refrigerator just before it reaches full doubling.

Unique flavors can be achieved by using alternatives to water in the sourdough, such as coffee. When using milk, the milk content in baked goods or other dishes can be increased, contributing to a richer flavor. Wheat sourdough fermented with milk has an especially mild taste.

The same principles apply to spelt sourdough as to wheat sourdough. Suitable flours for refreshing include Type-630 spelt flour and 1050. Whole spelt flour can also be used, but over time, it tends to develop more acidic flavors.

COMMON SOURDOUGH METHODS

The mildest and fastest method for refreshing sourdough starter is the **1:1:1 method**. This is also well suited for baking. This method involves mixing 1 part wheat starter + 1 part warm water + 1 part wheat flour and allowing it to ferment at a warm temperature of 79–86 °F (26–30 °C). The mixture should double in volume within 2–4 hours. This method is often used for pure sourdough breads without added yeast. To ensure strong fermentation activity, it is advisable to refresh the wheat starter one or two additional times beforehand, so that the sourdough has a good leavening power.

Example 1:1:1
> 50 g wheat starter
> 50 g warm water (104°F [40°C])
> 50 g Type-550 or Type-1050 all-purpose flour

Thoroughly mix everything in a clean jar (with a lid) and close the lid loosely.

Let the mixture ferment in a warm place 79–86 °F (26–30 °C) for about 2–4 hours.

Other mild fermentation methods for refreshing or baking include ratios ranging from **1:2:2** to **1:5:5**. The fermentation time must be adjusted based on the surrounding temperature and the chosen ratio of starter, water, and flour. The less starter used in relation to flour and water, the longer the fermentation time. The timing also depends on the activity of the individual starter culture.

Example 1:2:2
> 20 g wheat starter
> 40 g warm water (104°F [40°C])
> 40 g Type-550 or Type-1050 all-purpose flour

Thoroughly mix the wheat starter with the warm water and flour. Cover and let ferment at 79–86 °F [26–30 °C]) for 4–6 hours.

A single-stage fermentation method with a 1:10:10 ratio is also possible. Due to the longer and cooler fermentation time, this method usually results in a more pronounced acidity compared to the previously mentioned techniques. In this method, mix 1 part wheat starter + 10 parts warm water + 10 parts wheat flour and leave to ferment at room temperature for 10–12 hours. If the sourdough culture is highly active, fermentation can occur much faster. For better time management, the amount of starter can be halved, for example, when fermenting overnight.

Example 1:10:10
> 10 g wheat starter
> 100 g warm water (104°F [40°C])
> 100 g Type-550 or Type-1050 all-purpose flour

Thoroughly mix everything in a clean jar (with a lid) and close the lid loosely.

Let the mixture ferment at room temperature 72 °F (22 °C) for 10–12 hours.

CONVERTING WHEAT SOURDOUGH TO LIEVITO MADRE OR RYE SOURDOUGH

Wheat sourdough → Rye sourdough
> 10 g wheat starter
> 50 g warm water (104°F [40°C])
> 50 g Type-1050 high-gluten flour

Thoroughly mix everything in a clean jar (with a lid) and close the lid loosely.

Let the mixture ferment in a warm place 79–82 °F (26–28 °C) until it has doubled in volume

Afterward, continue refreshing it like a rye sourdough (see page 20). At least five refreshments are needed before the sourdough culture is fully converted.

Wheat sourdough → Lievito Madre

> 50 g wheat starter
> 10 g warm water (104°F [40°C])
> 50 g Type-550 wheat flour

Dissolve the wheat starter in the water, then knead thoroughly with the flour.

Place the mixture in a clean jar with a lid, close the lid loosely, and let it ferment in a warm place at 79–86 °F (26–30 °C) until it has doubled in volume.

Then continue refreshing it as Lievito Madre (see page 25). Up to five refreshments are required to fully transition the sourdough culture.

European Flour to US Flour Conversion Chart

European Type	US Equivalent
Type-405	Pastry Flour
Type-550	All-Purpose Flour
Type-812	Bread Flour
Type-1050	High-Gluten Flour
Type-1150	Rye Flour
Type-1600	White Whole Wheat Flour
Type-1700	Whole Wheat Flour
Type-00	Italian 00 Flour
Type 1800	Pumpernickel Flour
Type-630	White Spelt Flour
Roggen-Vollkornmehl	Pumpernickel Flour
Dinkel-Vollkornmehl	Whole Spelt Flour

Mature rye and wheat sourdough (from top to bottom).

24 ARTISAN SOURDOUGH: BREAD AND BEYOND

LIEVITO MADRE

Lievito Madre is a firm wheat sourdough with a mild aroma, abundant sourdough yeasts, and exceptional leavening power. In Italy, it is often referred to as "Pasta Madre" or "Lievito Naturale." A famous Italian classic made with this sourdough is panettone. But bread dough, ciabatta or focaccia are also often made with it. In France, a similar firm wheat sourdough is known as "Levain Dur." Aside from bread, Lievito Madre—whether freshly refreshed or straight from the fridge—can enhance both sweet and savory dishes with its wonderful flavors.

KEY FACTS

Lievito Madre is a mild sourdough with good leavening power, making it ideal for light, Mediterranean, and sweet baked goods such as rolls, pizza, or yeast pastries.

Characteristic of Lievito Madre is the refreshment with a low water content and a large amount of starter as well as a short fermentation time at warm temperatures.

There is usually only 40–50 g of water per 100 g of wheat flour. This is why we are talking about a solid sourdough. The exact amount of water needed for refreshment depends on the flour—some absorb more, some less. The consistency of the kneaded sourdough is reminiscent of marzipan. With Type-550 wheat flour, a ratio of 50 g water to 100 g flour usually works perfectly.

The classic flours for refreshing Lievito Madre are, for example, the Type-0 or Type-00 Italian wheat flours, but Type-550 wheat flour (W 700 in Austria) is also excellent. Type-1050 wheat flour also works, but traditionally the use of very light flours is used. Type-1050 wheat flour can help revitalize a somewhat inactive culture due to its higher nutrient content. In most cases, simply refreshing Lievito Madre several times with the usual flour will restore its strength.

For long, cold fermentation, a mild Lievito Madre works well. If fermentation lasts an exceptionally long time without added yeast, the sour flavors may become more pronounced.

The mixing ratio of the ingredients in Lievito Madre is usually always the same, both for refreshing and for baking.

Before **mixing Lievito Madre** into dough, it should have at least doubled or even tripled in volume. Some baking enthusiasts also measure the pH. This should then be approximately ± 4.3.

When refreshing the Lievito Madre, it should be placed in the refrigerator once it has nearly doubled, or at the latest, when it has doubled.

Using milk instead of water for refreshment can increase the milk content in baked goods, enhancing their richness. This can be particularly beneficial for sweet baked goods. Since milk is not 100% water, the sourdough may become slightly firmer, so the liquid amount is often slightly increased when using milk.

Lievito Madre can also be maintained with Type-630 spelt flour, creating a firm and mild spelt sourdough, or **Spelt Lievito Madre**.

TYPICAL SOURDOUGH REFRESHMENT

The usual mixing ratio for refreshing is the 1:0.5:1 method. It is commonly used for both care and baking. This involves 1 part Lievito Madre starter 0.5 parts warm water whipped until foamy and then thoroughly kneaded with 1 part wheat flour to form a smooth dough and left to ferment at 79–86 °F (26–30 °C). The mixture should double in volume within 2–4 hours.

For pure sourdough baking without added yeast, it is recommended to refresh Lievito Madre at least once beforehand to ensure maximum activity and leavening strength.

Example

> 50 g Lievito Madre starter
> 20–25 g warm water (104°F [40°C])
> 50 g Type-550 wheat flour

Whisk the Lievito Madre starter and water until frothy. Then knead thoroughly with the flour. Cover and let ferment in a warm place at 79–86 °F (26–30 °C) for **2–4 hours**.

CONVERTING LIEVITO MADRE TO LIQUID WHEAT SOURDOUGH OR RYE SOURDOUGH

Note: Converting Lievito Madre to liquid wheat sourdough is not strictly necessary for the recipes in this book. It can simply be refreshed using the 1:1:1 method and used immediately as a liquid wheat sourdough.

For example: 50 g Lievito Madre starter + 50 g warm water + 50 g Type-550 wheat flour results in a slightly firmer texture but remains within the typical range for wheat sourdough, essentially creating Li.co.li.

Lievito Madre → Liquid wheat sourdough

> 50 g Lievito Madre starter
> 50–70 g warm water (104°F [40°C])
> 50 g Type-550 or Type-1150 wheat flour

Whisk the Lievito Madre starter and water until frothy. Then mix with the wheat flour. Place in a clean jar with a loose lid and let ferment in a warm place at 79–86 °F (26–30 °C) warm location until doubled.

Then, continue refreshing it as a wheat sourdough (see page 21). The sourdough can be used immediately. Up to five refreshments may be necessary until the sourdough culture is completely converted, especially when changing flour.

Lievito Madre → Rye sourdough

> 50 g Lievito Madre starter
> 70 g warm water (104°F [40°C])
> 50 g Type-1050 rye flour

Whisk the Lievito Madre starter and water until frothy. Then mix with the rye flour. Place in a clean jar with a loose lid and let ferment in a warm place at 79–82 °F (26–28 °C) warm location until doubled.

Afterward, continue refreshing it like a rye sourdough (see page 19). At least five refreshments are needed before the sourdough culture is fully converted.

SPECIAL FORM: SWEET SOURDOUGH

To prepare a firm wheat sourdough for leavening heavy doughs without added yeast, it can be refreshed several times with the addition of sugar (about 20% of the flour weight). Fermentation will initially take noticeably longer than usual.

Since a higher sugar concentration in sweet yeast doughs binds free water (hygroscopic effect) and creates less favorable conditions for microorganism reproduction, sugar inhibits fermentation. (That is why sugar is also used to preserve food.)

By refreshing sourdough with added sugar, the microbial flora in the sourdough becomes accustomed to the "challenging" conditions, encouraging the growth of microorganisms that later thrive in sugar-rich doughs and are capable of leavening heavy, sugary doughs.

Since heavy doughs can also be successfully leavened with a well-refreshed Lievito Madre, and maintaining an additional sweet sourdough over time requires significant effort and resources; this book does not include recipes for sweet sourdough. Maintaining such a sourdough is only worthwhile for those who frequently prepare sweet and heavy yeast doughs.

PRESERVING SOURDOUGH

There are various methods to preserve sourdough for an extended period, such as before going on vacation or when baking will not be possible for a while. These methods can also serve as a backup—a safeguard for one's sourdough culture.

If necessary, this backup can then be reactivated. The "need" sometimes occurs faster than expected: a jar of sourdough may fall and break, mold might develop, or the sourdough may accidentally be entirely used up in baking.

> **The basic principle of preservation is the removal of water. The less free water available to the microorganisms in the sourdough, the less active they are, and the slower they consume nutrients. With all preservation methods, several refreshments will be required after reactivation to restore the original activity level.**

1. FEEDING HARDER THAN USUAL

If sourdough cannot be fed for an extended period, it should be prepared in advance. Then, after a long period without refreshing, it will be active again even more quickly and ready for baking. The aim is to slow down the metabolism of the microorganisms so that the food lasts as long as possible, ideally for the entire period. The sourdough will last for a few weeks if stored in the refrigerator.

Example: Rye sourdough

Firmer refresher:
Mix 20 g starter + 25–30 g water (104°F [40°C]) + 50 g rye flour thoroughly and leave to ferment as usual. However, as soon as the volume has increased by about half, refrigerate (preferably 37 °F [3 °C]).

Refresher for reactivation:
Mix 25 g starter + 35–40 g water (104°F [40°C]) + 25 g flour and leave to ferment in a warm environment until activity is visible and the mixture is filled with air bubbles. Then refresh as usual.

2. CRUMBLED SOURDOUGH ("GERSTL")

For this method, the previously refreshed starter is mixed with enough flour to form a fine, crumbly texture resembling a crumble dough. The flour that is normally used for feeding is used for the sourdough culture.

The crumbly sourdough is then stored in the refrigerator and will keep there for several weeks to months. The flour provides nutrients for the microorganisms, while the low water content reduces their metabolism to a minimum. The reactivation of crumbly sourdough is usually better and faster than that of dry sourdough.

Preparation:
Mix the starter with enough flour until a crumbly texture forms, then refrigerate.

Reactivation:
Mix the crumb sourdough with enough water (104°F [40°C]) until a homogeneous mass is formed. Let it ferment in a warm environment until visible activity appears and the mixture is filled with air bubbles. Then, refresh as usual.

3. DRYING (DRIED SOURDOUGH)

This is the easiest way to preserve sourdough for a long time.

Preparation:

Spread the sourdough as thinly as possible onto a sheet of parchment paper or reusable baking foil and let it dry completely at room temperature. Firm sourdough (Lievito Madre) should be rolled out as thinly as possible.

Drying takes about 1–2 days. Alternatively, the drying process can be accelerated in the oven, but the temperature must not exceed 104 °F (40 °C), otherwise the microorganisms will die and the dry sourdough can no longer be reactivated. Complete drying is essential to prevent mold formation.

The sourdough can then be crumbled or ground into powder. Stored in an airtight, light-protected container, this dried sourdough can last for several years.

Reactivation:

Mix 20 g water (104°F [40°C]) + 10 g dried sourdough + 10 g flour and let ferment in a warm environment until visible activity appears and the mixture is filled with air bubbles. Then refresh as usual.

4. ROASTED SOURDOUGH (RÖSTSAUERTEIG)

Roasted sourdough, also known as "Fleur de Levain," is more of a way to reuse sourdough rather than a preservation method and is a special form of dried sourdough. Due to heat exposure, roasted sourdough can be reactivated.

The appeal of roasted sourdough lies primarily in its interesting and complex flavors. At the same time, the acidity decreases during roasting. When rye sourdough is roasted, particularly intense aromas are created. The shelf life of roasted sourdough is basically unlimited.

Preparation:

As with dried sourdough, spread the sourdough as thinly as possible onto a sheet of parchment paper or reusable baking foil, but instead of air drying, roast it in the oven. Firm sourdough (Lievito Madre) should be rolled out as thinly as possible.

Lower temperatures produce mild roasted aromas, while higher temperatures create more intense flavors. The residual heat of the oven after baking is well-suited for this process. The sourdough must be completely dried during roasting. Once cooled, it can be ground into a powder using a blender or mortar.

IDEAS FOR USING DRIED AND ROASTED SOURDOUGH

- Replace 10–20 g of flour in a bread or roll dough (based on 500 g flour) with roasted sourdough.

- Use pure or mixed with flour for dusting dough surfaces.

- Use pure or mixed with flour to dust proofing baskets or greased loaf pans.

- Sprinkle on dough pieces before baking—best applied to slightly moistened surfaces.

- Replace part of the flour for a flour dough.

- Mix with breadcrumbs for breading, buttered crumbs on vegetables like asparagus, or as a binder for meat mixtures such as meatballs.

- Add 1 tsp.–1 Tbsp. to soups, sauces, and savory dishes for flavoring and thickening.

IDEAS FOR USING STARTER DISCARD

- Use as a thickener for sauces and soups.
- Make a sourdough spread by mixing it with water.
- Use as a base for a flour dough.
- Add to bread doughs as an aromatic dough component (adjusting flour and water accordingly).

Dried sourdough, crumbled sourdough, and roasted sourdough (from top to bottom).

SIDE NOTE ON BREAD BAKING

Baking bread, rolls, and pastries such as braided bread is usually divided into the following important steps.

1. PREPARING PRE-DOUGHS
Depending on the recipe, pre-doughs are made first. These include sourdoughs in particular, but also starter doughs, swelling pieces, scalding pieces, and flourdoughs.

2. PREPARING DOUGH
Before kneading, there's often a short hydration phase called autolyse or fermentolyse. In autolyse, only liquids and flour are mixed. Fermentolyse also includes sourdough preferments (a mixture of flour, water, and yeast, like a starter), which means it needs less resting time.

Typically, wet ingredients go into the mixing bowl first. Very small quantities of yeast are preferably dissolved in the bulk liquid first. This is followed by the dry ingredients.

Machine kneading generally consists of a longer mixing phase at low speed, followed by a shorter phase at higher speed to properly develop the gluten network. The final dough should pass the **windowpane test**. (Take a small piece of dough and slowly stretch it until it forms a thin, translucent membrane without tearing.) Rye or rye-mixed doughs are an exception here—they are only mixed and do not form a gluten structure, which is why a window test is not possible.

The alternative, kneading by hand, requires a lot of effort and is usually very time-consuming.

3. BULK FERMENTATION: THE FIRST DOUGH REST
During this initial resting phase, microorganisms begin their activity, and fermentation starts. At the same time, the flour components continue to swell with the liquid.

For the bulk fermentation, the dough is placed in a lightly oiled bowl or dough tray (rectangular, food-safe plastic container with a lid) and then covered. Neutral-flavored oils work best for greasing.

During the bulk fermentation, the doughs (with the exception of rye or rye-mixed doughs) are **stretched and folded** once or several times with moistened hands. This gives the doughs significantly more structure and makes them firmer and easier to shape later on thanks to the firming. In addition, oxygen and CO^2 are exchanged and the activity of microorganisms is stimulated.

4. SHAPING
Shaping tightens the dough and gives it its final form. Bread doughs are typically shaped into round or elongated loaves. Small dough pieces are often rounded in a process called "round tightening."

Shaping is usually done on a lightly floured surface. Rye flour, durum wheat flour, or fine wheat/spelt semolina work particularly well. It's crucial to incorporate as little extra flour as possible to prevent flour pockets from forming in the crumb later.

5. BULK FERMENTATION: FINAL PROOFING/SECOND RISE

This is the last fermentation phase of the shaped dough before baking. During this stage, the volume should increase sufficiently to ensure optimal oven spring and crumb structure. The dough can be left to rise with the dough seam (dough closure) created during shaping facing downwards or upwards and usually takes place in a floured proving basket or baker's linen/kitchen towel.

Poke test: In addition to observing the increase in volume, the so-called poke test is used to assess how far the maturation of a dough piece has progressed. This makes particular sense for wheat and spelt doughs or wheat and spelt mixed doughs. The dough surface is pressed with the lightly floured or moistened fingertip (index finger) to a depth of about 0.5–1 cm. The less and slower the dent that has formed fills up again, the further the dough proofing has progressed.

If the dough has nearly doubled in size, feels elastic, soft, and airy, and the indentation from the finger test slowly and only partially refills, the dough is at the ideal stage. It will have an excellent oven spring, good volume, and a nicely developed crust. If the dough has at least doubled, feels soft and sponge-like with a slight tension, and the indentation remains nearly unchanged, it has reached **full proof**. Oven spring will be minimal, and the baked goods will not split, which is desirable for items like burger buns.

6. BAKING

Baking should begin as soon as the dough reaches the desired proofing stage. It is recommended to bake bread, rolls, and similar baked goods in a domestic oven on a thick baking stone (15–30 mm) or baking steel (steel plate with 6–8 mm). Due to their excellent heat storage and direct heat transfer to the dough, these ensure good oven rise, provided they are well preheated.

If baking with the seam side down, the dough is usually scored with a sharp blade (lame or knife), cutting 3–5 mm deep in one decisive motion. If baking with the seam up, the dough will naturally split open in a rustic way.

The process of placing the ripe dough into the oven is called **"shooting."** This is best done with a bread peel, thin wooden board, or rimless baking sheet.

Steaming: Steam is essential during the first minutes of baking. It condenses on the dough's surface, keeping it flexible and allowing for expansion. To do this, place a shallow tray or pan on the bottom rack of your oven. When you're ready to put your bread in the oven, pour hot water into the tray to create steam. You can also create steam by using ice cubes or a Dutch oven.

If you are unsure whether a piece is fully baked, you can measure the **core temperature** with a probe thermometer. For bread and rolls this should be 201–208 °F (94–98 °C) and for fine pastries 198–201 °F (92–94 °C).

GUIDE TO THE RECIPES

- The **activity of your own sourdough** starter plays a major role and can lead to different fermentation times than those specified in the recipe.

- **41 °F (5 °C)–degree rule:** Just 41 °F (5 °C) more than the recipe calls for halves the fermentation time, 41 °F (5 °C) less than the recipe calls for doubles it.

- The term **"room temperature"** is assumed to be **72 °F (22 °C)**.

- The term **"cool water"** refers to tap water at around **59 °F (15 °C)**

- Cheap supermarket flour in particular is often of poorer quality with lower water absorption.

- Initially, **hold back 10–20% of the specified liquid** and add it gradually if needed.

- The listed kneading times are guidelines and may vary depending on the mixer.

- Check the dough temperature in time and perform the windowpane test (page 30) for wheat and spelt doughs.

- The timetables shown represent a possible timeline. The dough preparation time is generally assumed to be 20–30 minutes. Resting, fermentation, and baking times are highlighted in bold for easier planning.

- For recipes in this book that require a larger amount of starter, you can use freshly fed sourdough if there isn't enough starter available.

- Recipes that allow for the use of leftovers are marked accordingly.

TIP: BAKING BREAD IN A POT/DUTCH OVEN

If the loaves of bread are to be baked in a cast iron pot or Dutch oven instead of free-standing as in the recipe, the pot must first be preheated to 482 °F (250 °C) top/bottom heat. Then, carefully turn the dough from the proofing basket into the hot pot, cover with the lid, and bake at 482 °F (250 °C) top/bottom heat for 20 minutes. After 20 minutes, remove the lid, reduce the temperature to 410 °F (210 °C), and finish baking the bread in 10–15 minutes.

Metric to Imperial Conversion Chart

Metric	Imperial
1 g	.04 oz
5 g	.25 oz
10 g	.35 oz
15 g	.50 oz
20 g	.70 oz
25 g	1.00 oz
30 g	1.06 oz
35 g	1.23 oz
40 g	1.40 oz
50 g	2.00 oz
60 g	2.12 oz
70 g	2.47 oz
80 g	2.82 oz
90 g	3.17 oz
100 g	3.50 oz
120 g	4.23 oz

Metric	Imperial
125 g	4.41 oz
130 g	4.59 oz
140 g	4.94 oz
150 g	5.30 oz
160 g	5.64 oz
175 g	6.17 oz
180 g	6.35 oz
200 g	7.00 oz
230 g	8.11 oz
240 g	8.46 oz
250 g	8.82 oz
300 g	10.60 oz
350 g	12.35 oz
400 g	14.11 oz
450 g	15.87 oz
500 g	17.64 oz

ESSENTIAL TOOLS FOR SOURDOUGH BAKING

To get started, you'll need a few essential tools. Having the right equipment will make your baking experience smoother and more enjoyable:

- **Kitchen Scale:** Precision is key in sourdough baking. **Our recipes use the most precise method of measurement, so a kitchen scale is a must-have.** It ensures that all ingredients are measured accurately, just as they were when we tested the recipes. Ingredients are primarily given in grams, as this is the most precise way to measure.

- **Mixing Bowls:** A set of large mixing bowls for combining ingredients and allowing the dough to rise.

- **Bench Scraper:** Useful for handling and shaping the dough.

- **Proofing Basket:** Helps the dough maintain its shape during the final rise.

- **Dutch Oven or Baking Stone:** Essential for creating the perfect crust by trapping steam during baking.

- **Lame or Sharp Knife:** For scoring the dough before baking, which allows it to expand properly in the oven.

- **Thermometer:** To check the internal temperature of your bread, ensuring it's fully baked.

- **Spurtle:** A versatile tool for mixing and stirring dough, especially useful for incorporating ingredients evenly.

- **Danish Bread Whisk:** Ideal for mixing dough without overworking it, thus achieving the perfect texture.

PRECISION IN MEASUREMENTS

In this cookbook, all measurements are listed exactly as they were measured during our recipe testing. This means you can trust that following the instructions precisely will yield the best results. Using a kitchen scale to measure ingredients by weight rather than volume ensures consistency and accuracy, which is especially important in sourdough baking.

Use a kitchen scale while following these recipes to get the most accurate measurements.

Makes 8 Slices | Lievito Madre

NAAN BREAD

Naan is a flatbread from Asia that is usually served as a side dish to warm dishes such as curry. It is traditionally baked in a tandoori oven.

TOTAL TIME	PREPARATION TIME	FERMENTATION TIME
6.5–9.5 hours	1 hour	2–4 hours (sourdough) + 4.5 hours (total dough)

FOR THE LIEVITO MADRE
60 g Lievito Madre starter
30 g warm water (104°F [40°C])
60 g Type-550 wheat flour

FOR THE DOUGH
250 g of cool water
50 g cold whole milk yogurt
Mature Lievito Madre
3 g fresh yeast (optional)
5 g liquid honey
400 g Type-550 wheat flour
12 g salt
10 g olive oil

ADDITIONAL ITEMS
Neutral vegetable oil for the bowl
Flour for working

1. Whisk the Lievito Madre starter with the warm water until frothy. Then, knead thoroughly with the flour. Cover the Lievito Madre and allow it to ferment at 79–86 °F (26–30 °C) for 2–4 hours until it has doubled in size.

2. For the dough, mix all the ingredients except for the salt and olive oil in a kitchen or dough mixer on low speed for **10 minutes**. Then, add the salt and knead the dough on a higher speed for **3–5 minutes**, adding the olive oil in two or three portions and kneading it in.
   Dough weight: approx. 880 g
   Dough temperature after kneading: approx. 75–79 °F (24–26 °C)

Bulk fermentation

3. Let the dough rise in a lightly oiled bowl, covered, at room temperature for about **3 hours** until it has doubled in size.

Shaping

4. Divide the dough into eight pieces of about 110 g each on a floured work surface and shape them loosely into rounds. Cover the dough pieces and let them rest for about **20 minutes**. Then, carefully stretch them into oval-shaped flatbreads about 8 inches (20 cm) long, keeping the outer edge slightly thicker.

Final proof

5. Let the dough flats rest, covered (e.g., with a kitchen towel), at room temperature for about **60–80 minutes**.

FOR THE TOPPING

1 garlic clove

30 g butter or ghee (clarified butter)

2 Tbsp. chopped parsley or chopped cilantro

> **TIP**
> Covering the flatbreads with a kitchen towel will help keep them warm and soft for longer.

6. For the topping, peel the garlic and chop finely. Melt the butter in a saucepan. Add the garlic and keep the garlic butter mixture warm until ready to use.

Baking

7. Preheat a cast iron pan without fat on the stove at a medium-to-high temperature. Remove excess flour from the dough. Cook the dough pieces one by one in the pan, flipping them when the bottom turns golden brown and the top starts to form bubbles. Then, remove the naan breads from the pan and immediately spread with the warm garlic butter. Sprinkle the naan breads with parsley and serve.

Makes 8 Tortillas (8–10 inches [20–25 cm] diameter) | Wheat Starter

WHEAT TORTILLAS

Tortillas—these very thin flatbreads cooked in the pan are a popular base in Tex-Mex cuisine for burritos and quesadillas, or they are often rolled with fillings into wraps.

TOTAL TIME	PREPARATION TIME	RESTING TIME
50–60 minutes	30–40 minutes	20 minutes

FOR THE DOUGH

300 g wheat starter
50 g cool water
250 g Type "405 wheat flour + more for working
15 g olive oil
5 g salt

1. Knead all ingredients together into a smooth dough.
   Dough weight: 620 g

2. Divide the dough into eight pieces of about 75–80 g each. Shape them into round forms and let them rest covered for about **20 minutes**.

3. Then, roll each dough piece into a circle about 8–10 inches (20–25 cm) in diameter. If the dough shrinks again, cover and let it rest for another **15 minutes** and then roll it out again.

4. Preheat a cast-iron pan without fat on the stove at a medium-to-high temperature. Remove excess flour from the rolled-out dough. Cook each tortilla one by one in the pan for about **1 minute** on each side. They should not get too dark, or they will become dry.

5. Then serve the wheat tortillas immediately or cover them with a slightly damp kitchen towel to keep them soft. Or, store the tortillas in an airtight container.

TIP

Instead of 300 g wheat starter, Lievito Madre can also be used. For this, thoroughly mix 225 g Lievito Madre starter with 75 g water before making the dough.

Makes 3–4 servings | Lievito Madre

POTATO GNOCCHI

These small Italian dumplings made from boiled potatoes and durum wheat flour can be served as a side dish or as a main course.

TOTAL TIME	PREPARATION TIME	COOKING TIME
1 hour	20 minutes	20–40 minutes + 2–3 minutes

FOR THE DOUGH

800 g waxy potatoes
150 g Lievito Madre starter
150 g durum wheat flour + more for working
1 egg yolk
5–8 g salt + more for cooking

1. Wash the potatoes thoroughly and then cook them with the skin on for **20–40 minutes**, depending on their size. Then drain, rinse with cold water, and peel. While still warm, press the potatoes through a potato ricer (alternatively, mash them with a potato masher). Allow the potatoes to cool uncovered.

2. Tear the Lievito Madre starter into small pieces (this will make it easier to mix with the potatoes later) and add it to the potatoes. Also add the durum wheat flour, egg yolk, and salt. Quickly knead everything with your hands to form a smooth, supple, and malleable dough. If the mixture is still too soft and sticky, add some durum wheat flour.

3. Flour the work surface generously with durum wheat flour and shape the dough into ropes about ½ inch (2 cm) in diameter. Cut these with a knife into pieces about ½ inch (2 cm) wide. Either pull each piece over a floured gnocchi board or roll it over the back of a fork. This creates the typical gnocchi grooves.

4. Bring salted water to a boil in a large pot. Drop the gnocchi into the lightly simmering water and let them cook for about **2–3 minutes** (don't let it boil). They are ready when they float to the surface. Then, use a slotted spoon to lift them out of the water and serve immediately.

TIP

Gnocchi can also be made in advance and frozen. For this, mix the freshly formed raw gnocchi with some durum wheat flour and freeze them airtight or lightly vacuum-sealed. To serve, drop the frozen gnocchi into boiling salted water and cook until they float to the surface.

Makes 4 Servings | Wheat Starter

SPÄTZLE

A basic recipe for the typical Central European pasta—as a side dish or for further processing into cheese spaetzle.

TOTAL TIME
45 minutes

PREPARATION TIME
30 minutes

RESTING TIME
15 minutes

FOR THE DOUGH
200 g wheat starter
5 medium eggs
200 g Type-550 wheat flour
100 g durum wheat semolina (alternatively wheat flour)
5 g salt + more for cooking

1. Briefly mix the wheat starter and the eggs. Then add the wheat flour, durum wheat semolina, and salt. Stir the dough with a wooden spoon until it is smooth and bubbling. If the dough flows slowly from the spoon without tearing, it has the right consistency.

2. Cover the dough and let it rest at room temperature for about **15 minutes**.

3. Next, bring salted water to a boil in a large pot. Scrape the spaetzle dough in portions from a board into the boiling water (this is the traditional method). Or, put the dough into the water using a spaetzle press or a spaetzle slicer. Cook the spaetzle until they float on the surface of the water. Then remove with a slotted spoon and keep warm until all the dough has been processed. It is important to remove the finished spaetzle—if the raw dough for the next batch falls onto the cooked spaetzle in the pot, the two will stick together.

4. Serve the spaetzle immediately; if not eaten right away, rinse with cold water, drain thoroughly, and freeze after cooling.

TIP
Instead of 200 g wheat starter, Lievito Madre starter can also be used. For this, mix 150 g Lievito Madre starter with 50 g milk or water before making the dough.

Makes 4 Servings | Lievito Madre

FRESH PASTA

This dough is used for making fresh pasta, such as tagliatelle, fettuccine, or lasagna sheets. It is also excellent as a base for tortellini or ravioli.

TOTAL TIME	PREPARATION TIME	RESTING TIME
1 hour	30 minutes	30 minutes

FOR THE DOUGH
150 g Lievito Madre starter
200 g durum wheat flour + more for working and as needed
2 medium eggs
½ tsp. salt + more for cooking

1. Knead all ingredients into a smooth and supple but firm dough; depending on the size of the eggs, you may need 10–20 g more durum wheat flour if necessary. Cover the dough and let it rest at room temperature for about **30 minutes**.

2. After resting, knead the dough again or fold it a few times to make it more elastic. Lightly flour with durum wheat flour and roll out one-quarter of the dough as thin as possible using a rolling pin or a pasta machine. If using a pasta machine, start at setting 0 and roll the dough through several times until it reaches setting 6 (1.2 mm).

3. For fresh pasta, dust the pasta sheets with durum wheat flour, roll them up, and cut them into narrow (for fettuccine) or slightly wider strips (for tagliatelle) with a knife. Alternatively, run the pasta sheets through a fettuccine cutter; sometimes the dough cuts better if it is allowed to dry for **30 minutes** beforehand.

4. Loosen the freshly cut pasta and place it on a kitchen towel dusted with durum wheat flour. Bring salted water to a boil in a pot and cook the pasta until al dente, about **1–3 minutes**. Then, serve immediately or continue processing.

5. For lasagna, leave the pasta sheets to dry for **1 hour** before layering the casserole.

TIP
For a larger amount of pasta per serving, you can add 1 medium egg and 100 g durum wheat flour to the dough.

Makes 4 Servings | Rye Starter

SPELT PASTA

This pasta uses a dough with eggs made from spelt with whole grain content. It goes particularly well with savory sauces.

TOTAL TIME	PREPARATION TIME	RESTING TIME
1 hour	30 minutes	30 minutes

FOR THE DOUGH
100 g mild rye starter
100 g spelt whole grain flour
150 g spelt semolina + more for working and as needed
2 medium eggs
½ tsp. salt + more for cooking

1. Knead all ingredients into a smooth and supple but firm dough; depending on the size of the eggs, you may need 10–20 g more spelt semolina. Cover the dough and let it rest at room temperature for about **30 minutes**.

2. After resting, knead the dough again or fold it a few times to make it more elastic. Lightly flour with spelt semolina and roll out one quarter of the dough as thin as possible using a rolling pin or a pasta machine. If using a pasta machine, start at setting 0 and roll the dough through several times until it reaches setting 6 (1.2 mm).

3. Dust the pasta sheets with spelt semolina, roll them up, and cut them into narrow (for fettuccine) or slightly wider strips (for tagliatelle) with a knife. Alternatively, run the pasta sheets through a fettuccine cutter; sometimes the dough cuts better if it is allowed to dry for **30 minutes** beforehand.

4. Loosen the freshly cut pasta and place it on a kitchen towel dusted with spelt semolina. Bring salted water to a boil in a pot and cook the pasta until al dente, about **1–3 minutes**. Then serve immediately.

TIP
For a larger amount of pasta per serving, you can add 1 medium egg and 100 g spelt semolina to the dough.

Makes 4–6 Crêpes | Wheat Starter

HERB CRÊPES

*A recipe for savory pancakes with fresh herbs as a base for a hearty filling.
For neutral crêpes, the herbs and pepper can be left out.*

TOTAL TIME	PREPARATION TIME	FERMENTATION TIME
2.5–4.5 hours	30 minutes	2–4 hours

FOR THE MILK SOURDOUGH
100 g wheat starter
100 g warm whole milk (104°F [40°C])
100 g Type-405 wheat flour

FOR THE DOUGH
3 medium eggs
50 g whole milk
Mature milk sourdough
½ tsp. salt
1 pinch freshly ground black pepper
½ bunch of parsley
½ bunch of chives

ADDITIONAL ITEMS
Butter for frying

1. Dissolve the wheat starter in the warm milk and then mix thoroughly with the wheat flour. Cover the milk sourdough and allow it to ferment at 79–86 °F (26–30 °C) for **2–4 hours** until it has doubled in size.

2. For the dough, whisk the eggs with the milk, mature milk sourdough, salt, and pepper until well combined.

3. Wash the herbs and pat dry.

4. Finely chop the parsley and cut the chives into fine rolls. Mix both into the dough.

5. Heat the butter in a nonstick pan. Fry the dough in portions until golden brown on both sides to make crêpes. Then fill the crêpes as desired and serve.

TIP

The herb crêpes are also great as fritters or pancakes for a warming soup. To do this, cut the crêpes into strips, place them in a deep plate, and pour hot broth over them. If you want the dough to be a little thicker, you can leave out the whole milk.

Makes 8 Dumplings | Wheat Starter

SEMMELKNÖDEL (BREAD DUMPLINGS)

This specialty of southern German, Austrian, and Bohemian cuisine is traditionally served as a side with dishes like mushroom cream sauce, roast, or goulash.

TOTAL TIME	PREPARATION TIME	RESTING TIME	COOKING TIME
40 minutes	30 minutes	10 minutes	20 minutes

FOR THE DUMPLING DOUGH
5 stale bread rolls
(about 60 g each)
100 g whole milk
100 g wheat starter
1 large onion
20 g butter
2 medium eggs
1 tsp. salt + more for cooking
1 pinch freshly ground black pepper
2 Tbsp. chopped flat-leaf parsley
1 pinch grated nutmeg

1. Cut the bread rolls into small cubes and place them in a large bowl. Heat the milk until it steams and pour over the cubes. Then add the wheat starter and mix everything very well. Let the mixture soak for **10 minutes**.

2. Peel the onion and dice finely. Melt the butter in a pan and briefly sauté the onion cubes.

3. Mix the eggs with the salt and pepper, the chopped parsley, and a pinch of nutmeg. Add to the bread mixture together with the onion and knead well with your hands to form a dough.

4. Bring salted water to a boil in a large pot. With well-moistened hands, form tennis ball–sized dumplings from the dough, place them in the gently simmering water, and let them cook for about **20 minutes** (do not boil). The Semmelknödel dumplings are ready to serve once they float to the surface.

> **TIP**
> If the dumpling mixture is too soft and difficult to shape, mix in some breadcrumbs. If the mixture is too dry, add a little milk.

Makes 10–12 Dumplings | Lievito Madre

PALATINE-STYLE STEAMED DUMPLINGS

A different take on steamed dumplings: yeast dumplings steamed in a pan with a salty crust on the bottom. In the Palatinate region, they are traditionally served with potato soup and then enjoyed with vanilla or wine foam sauce.

TOTAL TIME	PREPARATION TIME	FERMENTATION TIME	COOKING TIME
6–8 hours	1 hour	2–4 hours + 2.5 hours	20–30 minutes

FOR THE FLOUR DOUGH
25 g Type-550 wheat flour
100 g whole milk

1. Mix the flour and milk in a small saucepan with a whisk until there are no lumps. Heat slowly and continue stirring. After a few minutes, the mixture begins to thicken like pudding. Remove from the heat and continue stirring for another **1–2 minutes**.

2. Then transfer the mixture and let it cool for a few minutes. Finally, cover the flour dough with cling film and leave to cool in the refrigerator.

FOR THE LIEVITO MADRE
30 g Lievito Madre starter
15 g warm water (104 °F [40 °C])
30 g Type-550 wheat flour

3. Whisk the Lievito Madre starter with the warm water until frothy. Then knead thoroughly with the flour. Let the Lievito Madre rise at 79–86 °F (26–30 °C) for **2–4 hours** until it doubles in volume.

FOR THE MAIN DOUGH
180–200 g cold whole milk
Cold flour dough
Mature Lievito Madre
10 g fresh yeast
30 g sugar
1 medium egg
425 g Type-550 wheat flour
30 g soft butter
5 g salt

4. For the main dough, mix 180 g of milk with the remaining ingredients—except for the butter and salt—using a stand mixer on low speed for **10 minutes**. Then add the butter and salt and knead on a higher speed for **5–8 minutes**. If necessary, incorporate the remaining milk while kneading.
   Dough weight: approx. 940 g
   Dough temperature after kneading: approx. 75–79 °F (24–26 °C)

ADDITIONAL ITEMS
Neutral vegetable oil for the bowl
Flour for working

FOR THE BROTH
Approx. 200 g of water
4 Tbsp. canola oil or clarified butter
2 pinches salt + more to taste

Bulk fermentation
5. Let the dough rise in a lightly oiled bowl at room temperature, covered, for **1.5 hours** until doubled in size, stretching and folding after **45 minutes**.

Shaping and final proof
6. On a floured surface, divide the dough into 10–12 pieces of about 80 g each and shape them into tight rounds. Let the dough pieces rise, covered, on the floured surface at room temperature for about **50–60 minutes**.

7. For the broth, bring approximately 100 g of water, the canola oil, and 1 pinch of salt (or more to taste) to a boil in a nonstick or cast-iron pan (at least 10 inches [26 cm] in diameter) with a high rim and a domed glass lid.

Cooking
8. Place five to six dough pieces into the pan using a spatula and immediately close the lid. Do not lift the lid from this point on!

9. Let everything come to a boil over high heat, then reduce to low to medium heat and simmer gently for about **20 minutes** until all the water has completely evaporated. If not fully evaporated, continue cooking on low heat until no liquid remains. There should also be hardly any condensation left on the lid of the pan. At this stage, the steamed dumplings should make crackling noises in the pan, which is when the golden-brown salt crust forms.

10. Once the steamed dumplings are cooked, lift the pan with the lid closed at an angle so that the remaining condensation drips down the side of the glass lid. Then remove the lid very carefully to prevent the condensation from dripping down. Remove the steamed dumplings and keep them warm in the oven.

11. Prepare the remaining dough pieces in the same way and then serve all the steamed dumplings immediately.

Makes 4 Small Waffles | Wheat Starter, Rye Starter, Lievito Madre

QUICK SOURDOUGH WAFFLES

Baking sourdough starter into waffles is a simple and quick way to use up leftover starter. These waffles can be served as a side with soups or dips and can also be fried in a pan instead of a waffle iron.

TOTAL TIME
10–15 minutes

FOR THE BASIC RECIPE
Clarified butter for greasing
200 g sourdough starter
2 pinches salt

OPTIONAL VARIATIONS
BASIC RECIPE AS DESIRED
1–2 tsp. soy sauce (omit salt from the base recipe)
1 tsp. white or black sesame seeds
½ tsp. dried herbs
1 tsp. chopped fresh herbs
4–8 tsp. grated cheese
2–3 tsp. crispy fried onions
1 pinch bread spice

1. Preheat a waffle iron and lightly grease it with clarified butter.

2. Mix the sourdough starter with salt first, then spoon the mixture into the center of the waffle iron, and bake into waffles. (You could also place the starter directly into the center of the waffle iron, and sprinkle the salt on top.)

3. Before baking, mix the sourdough starter with any of the optional ingredients or a combination of them.

> **TIP**
> Waffles made with wheat starter tend to be milder and more neutral in flavor. On the other hand, when made from rye starter, they taste much stronger and more like bread. Lievito Madre starter does not mix as easily with additional ingredients.

ARTISAN SOURDOUGH: BREAD AND BEYOND

Makes 2 Pancakes | Wheat Starter

HOBAK BUCHIMGAE WITH SESAME DIP SAUCE

These Korean zucchini pancakes are quick and easy to make. They can be served as a side dish, appetizer, or light main course.

TOTAL TIME	PREPARATION TIME	RESTING TIME
30 minutes	20 minutes	10 minutes

SESAME DIP SAUCE
1 garlic clove
2 Tbsp. soy sauce (Tamari or Shoyu)
1 Tbsp. mirin (rice wine; optional)
2 tsp. rice vinegar
1 tsp. toasted sesame oil
½ tsp. sugar
¼ tsp. gochugaru (Korean red chili flakes)

FOR THE DOUGH
250 g wheat starter
2 medium eggs
40 g rice flour
1 Tbsp. toasted sesame oil
1 tsp. salt
1 large zucchini (approx. 250 g)
2 scallions
1 green chili pepper (optional)

ADDITIONAL ITEMS
Canola oil for frying

1. Peel and finely chop the garlic. Mix together with the remaining ingredients and set the dipping sauce aside until serving.

2. For the dough, mix the wheat starter with the eggs well. Then stir in the rice flour, sesame oil, and salt. Cover the dough and let it rest for **10 minutes**.

3. Wash and clean the zucchini and cut it into fine julienne strips; if they are very juicy, squeeze them well. Wash and clean the spring onions and optionally the chili pepper and cut them into fine rings. Fold the zucchini, spring onions, and chili into the dough.

4. Heat the canola oil in a pan. Fry the batter in two portions, cooking each side until golden brown. Cut the finished zucchini pancakes into bite-size pieces and serve with the sesame dip sauce.

TIP
Instead of 250 g wheat starter, Lievito Madre starter can also be used. To do this, mix 190 g Lievito Madre starter with 60 g water thoroughly before preparing the dough.

PIZZA, QUICHE & CO.

Makes 1 Focaccia (deep baking sheet or oven dish, 14 x 10 inches [35 x 25 cm]) | Wheat Starter

FOCACCIA

This focaccia is a light, moist, and highly aromatic Italian-style flatbread. (See picture on page 60.)

TOTAL TIME	PREPARATION TIME	FERMENTATION TIME	TIME ON BAKING DAY
22–27 hours	45 minutes	2–3 hours (sourdough) + 19–23 hours (total dough)	1.5 hours

FOR THE WHEAT SOURDOUGH

50 g wheat starter (it should be very active and the last refreshment should not have been more than 12 hours ago. Better to refresh it again directly beforehand)
40 g warm water (104°F [40°C])
50 g Type-550 wheat flour

FOR THE AUTOLYSE DOUGH

350 g cool water
350 g Type-550 wheat flour
150 g Type-0 Manitoba flour (alternatively use Type-550 wheat flour, then use 10–20% less water)

FOR THE MAIN DOUGH

Mature wheat sourdough
Autolyse dough
12 g salt
15 g olive oil
40 g of cool water (as needed)

1. Thoroughly mix the wheat starter with the warm water and flour. Cover and let the wheat sourdough rise at 79–86 °F (26–30 °C) for **2–3 hours** until well doubled.

2. For the autolyse dough, briefly mix all ingredients and let rest, covered, at room temperature for **1 hour**.

3. For the main dough, add the wheat sourdough to the autolyse dough and knead in a stand mixer on low speed for **10 minutes**. Then add salt and olive oil, kneading on a higher setting for **3–5 more minutes**. Gradually knead in up to 40 g additional water as needed.
   Dough weight: approx. 1050 g
   Dough temperature after kneading: approx. 75–79 °F (24–26 °C)

THE DAY BEFORE

2:00 PM	3:00 PM	4:00 PM	5:20 PM	6:20 PM	7:20 PM
Prepare wheat sourdough	Mix the autolyse dough	Prepare the main dough	Stretch and fold	Stretch and fold	Stretch and fold

60   ARTISAN SOURDOUGH: BREAD AND BEYOND

ADDITIONAL ITEMS

Neutral vegetable oil for the bowl/container
Olive oil for working
1 tsp. dried oregano or 1 sprig rosemary with leaves removed
Fleur de Sel

Bulk fermentation and shaping

4. Cover the dough and leave to mature in a lightly oiled bowl or dough pan at 77–81 °F (25–27 °C) for a total of about **4 hours** until doubled, stretching and folding four times after **1, 2, 3, and 4 hours** respectively. Immediately after the fourth fold, place the dough, dough end down, either on a baking tray generously oiled with olive oil or in an oiled oven dish 14 x 10 inches (35 x 25 cm).

Final proof

5. Let the dough rest at room temperature, covered, for about **2 hours**, then transfer it to the refrigerator at 43–46 °F (6–8 °C) for about **12–16 hours** (check the temperature). Afterward, let it acclimate at room temperature for **1 hour**.

6. Sprinkle the dough with oregano and drizzle with a little olive oil. Using oiled fingertips, dimple the dough without deflating any air bubbles and gently stretch it toward the edges of the pan. Finally, sprinkle the dough with fleur de sel.

Baking

7. Preheat the oven to 446 °F (230 °C) top/bottom heat well in advance. Bake the focaccia in the lower third of the oven at 446 °F (230 °C) for about **30 minutes**. Then let it cool on a rack and serve.

8:20 PM
Stretch and fold onto baking sheet

10:20 PM
Put in the refrigerator

ON BAKING DAY

2:30 PM
Take out of the refrigerator

3:00 PM
Preheat oven

3:30 PM
Top and bake

4:00 PM
Remove from the oven

Focaccia (page 60).

Pinsa Romana (page 64).

Makes 4 Pieces | Lievito Madre

PINSA ROMANA

The Pinsa Romana, a modern invention, is reminiscent of pizza or focaccia. It is traditionally baked without any toppings and can then be topped as desired. (See picture on page 63.)

TOTAL TIME
54.5–78.5 hours

PREPARATION TIME
50 minutes

FERMENTATION TIME
53–77 hours (total dough)

TIME ON BAKING DAY
4.5 hours

FOR THE AUTOLYSE DOUGH

330 g cool water
250 g Type-550 wheat flour
150 g Type-0 Manitoba flour
(alternatively use Type-550 wheat flour, then use 10–20% less water)
50 g whole wheat flour

FOR THE MAIN DOUGH

1 g fresh yeast
30 g Lievito Madre starter
Autolyse dough
25 g rice flour
25 g chickpea flour (alternatively rice flour)
10 g salt
10 g olive oil
30 g cool water (as needed)

1. For the autolyse dough, mix all ingredients briefly but thoroughly and leave covered for **1 hour**.

2. For the final dough, add the fresh yeast and Lievito Madre starter to the autolyse dough and knead in a stand mixer on low speed for **1–2 minutes**. Then, add the rice flour and chickpea flour and knead on low speed for another **8 minutes**. Finally, add the salt and olive oil, then knead at a higher speed for **3–5 minutes**. If necessary, add up to 30 g of water.
   Dough weight: approx. 900 g
   Dough temperature after kneading: approx. 75–79 °F (24–26 °C)

DAY 1

2:00 PM
Mix the autolyse dough

3:00 PM
Prepare the main dough

4:20 PM
Stretch and fold + put in the refrigerator

DAY 4

2:00 PM
Take out of the fridge to make it round

4:00 PM
Preforming + final proof

5:30 PM
Preheat oven

ARTISAN SOURDOUGH: BREAD AND BEYOND

ADDITIONAL ITEMS
Neutral vegetable oil for the bowl/container
Rice flour for working
Olive oil for working

> **TIP**
> The recipe can also be baked very well with Type-0 pizza flour, which is suitable for a long dough maturation.

FOR THE TOPPING
12 cherry tomatoes
1 handful arugula
8 Tbsp. pesto verde or pesto rosso
4 Tbsp. black olives
Salt
Freshly ground black pepper
Olive oil for drizzling
Fresh basil leaves for sprinkling
Burrata, mozzarella, shaved Parmesan, or prosciutto (optional)

Bulk fermentation

3. Cover the dough in a lightly oiled bowl or dough tray and let it rise at room temperature for **1 hour**, then stretch and fold it. Transfer the dough to the refrigerator at 41 °F (5 °C) and let it ferment for **48–72 hours**.

Shaping and final proof

4. Divide the cold dough into four parts, each weighing about 225 g, and shape into a loose round shape. Cover the pieces and let them rest at room temperature for **2 hours**.

5. Then carefully roll out the dough pieces on plenty of rice flour to form long flatbreads about 8 inches (20 cm) long. Place two flatbreads each on a sheet of baking paper or baking foil and allow to rest, covered, for **2 hours**. Next, drizzle the dough pieces with a little olive oil and tap them a few times with oiled fingertips, stretching them to a length of about 10 inches (25 cm).

Baking

6. Preheat the oven to 482–536 °F (250–280 °C) top/bottom heat well in advance, (the hotter, the better).

7. Place the first dough pieces in the preheated oven and bake on the second shelf from the top for about **6–10 minutes**, depending on the temperature, with visual contact. Do the same with the remaining dough pieces.

8. Wash the tomatoes and cut them in half. Wash the arugula and pat dry. Spread the pesto on the baked pinsa, leaving a border of about ½ inch (2 cm) around the edges. Top with arugula, cherry tomatoes, and olives. Next, season with some salt and pepper and drizzle with a little olive oil. Then sprinkle with a few basil leaves. Sprinkle with burrata, mozzarella, shaved Parmesan, or top with Parma ham as desired. Serve the pinsa warm.

6:00 PM
Stretch + bake

6:10 PM
Remove from the oven + top

Makes 4 Pizzas | Lievito Madre

ITALIAN PIZZA

A recipe for an aromatic pizza with a thin crust and airy edges, just like the ones from the local Italian pizzeria. (See picture on page 66.)

TOTAL TIME	PREPARATION TIME	FERMENTATION TIME	TIME ON BAKING DAY
41–79 hours	40 minutes	2–4 hours (sourdough) + 38–74 hours (total dough)	1.5 hours

FOR THE LIEVITO MADRE
40 g Lievito Madre starter (it should be very active and the last refreshment should be no more than 12 hours ago; better to refresh it again beforehand)
20 g warm water (104°F [40°C])
40 g Type-550 wheat flour

FOR THE AUTOLYSE DOUGH
600 g Type-00 pizza flour (alternatively Type-550 wheat flour)
380–400 g water (depending on the water absorption of the flour)

FOR THE MAIN DOUGH
Mature Lievito Madre
Autolyse dough
12 g salt

1. Whisk the Lievito Madre starter with the water until frothy. Then knead with the flour. Cover the Lievito Madre and allow it to ferment at 79–86 °F (26–30 °C) for **2–4 hours** until it has doubled in size.

2. For the autolyse dough, mix all the ingredients briefly but thoroughly and let them rest, covered, for **20–30 minutes**.

3. For the main dough, add the mature Lievito Madre to the autolyse dough. Knead with a food processor/kneading machine on low speed for **8–10 minutes**. Then add the salt and knead at a higher speed for **4–8 minutes**.
   Dough weight: approx. 1,100 g
   Dough temperature after kneading: approx. 75–79 °F (24–26 °C)

DAY 1
4:00 PM
Prepare Lievito Madre

5:30 PM
Mix the autolyse dough

6:00 PM
Prepare the main dough

6:50 PM
Stretch and fold

7:20 PM
Form round shapes + refrigerate

DAY 3
4:30 PM
Take out of the refrigerator

ARTISAN SOURDOUGH: BREAD AND BEYOND

ADDITIONAL ITEMS

Neutral vegetable oil for the bowl/container
(Durum wheat) flour to work with

FOR THE TOPPING

400 g canned tomatoes
(preferably San Marzano)
2 pinches salt
400 g mozzarella or Fior di Latte,
olives, salami, or other toppings as desired

> **TIP**
>
> For a version with additional yeast, use only 60 g of refreshed Lievito Madre and add 1–2 g of fresh yeast to the main dough. Let the dough ferment at a slightly colder temperature of 41 °F (5 °C) in the fridge.

Bulk fermentation and ball proofing

4. Cover the dough and leave to rise in a lightly oiled bowl or dough pan at room temperature for **1 hour,** stretching and folding after **30 minutes**.

5. Then transfer the dough to a lightly floured surface and divide it into four equal portions of about 275 g each. Shape each portion into a round ball.

6. Place the dough balls into a greased container or a lightly oiled round bowl.

7. Let them ferment, covered, in the refrigerator at about 41–43 °F (5–6 °C) for a total of **36–72 hours**. (For very long fermentation times, shape the dough balls later, for example, after **24 or 36 hours**. Briefly remove the dough from the fridge, shape, and return to cold storage.) Then allow to acclimatize for at least **1 hour**.

Shaping

8. Remove the dough balls from the dough tray or bowl and place them on a work surface that has been well floured with durum wheat flour. Gently press a border around the edges with your fingertips. Then carefully pull and stretch the dough balls from the inside outwards (do not roll them out!). If the dough keeps shrinking, cover it and let it rest for **10–15 minutes**.

9. Drain the tomatoes from the can, then crush them and mix with the salt. Spread sparingly over the rolled out dough pieces. Cut the mozzarella into slices and spread on top. Top with olives, salami, or other ingredients as desired.

Baking

10. Preheat the oven as hot as possible, ideally to 536–572 °F (280–300 °C) top/bottom heat (the hotter, the better). Bake each pizza individually on the second rack from the top for about **4–10 minutes**, depending on the oven temperature.

5:00 PM
Preheat oven

5:30 PM
Shaping

5:40 PM
Top + bake

6:50 PM
Remove from the oven

Italian Pizza (page 66).

Crispy Pan Pizza (page 70).

Makes 1 Pizza (about 2 servings) | Wheat Sourdough Starter

CRISPY PAN PIZZA

Pizza with a difference: a crispy version with a thick, fluffy base from the pan, American style. (See picture on page 69.)

TOTAL TIME	PREPARATION TIME	FERMENTATION TIME	TIME ON BAKING DAY
33.5–59.5 hours	50 minutes	4–6 hours (sourdough) + 28–52 hours (total dough)	3.5 hours

FOR THE SOURDOUGH
10 g wheat starter
20 g warm water (104°F [40°C])
20 g Type-550 wheat flour

FOR THE FERMENTOLYSE DOUGH
150 g water
Mature sourdough
230 g Type-550 wheat flour

FOR THE MAIN DOUGH
1 g fresh yeast
Fermentolyse dough
5 g salt
10 g olive oil

1. Thoroughly mix the wheat starter with the warm water and flour. Cover and leave to ferment at 79–86 °F (26–30 °C) for **4–6 hours** until well doubled.

2. For the fermentolyse dough, briefly mix the water, sourdough, and wheat flour. Let the fermentolyse dough rest for **20–30 minutes**.

3. For the main dough, add the fresh yeast to the fermentolyse dough and knead with a stand mixer or dough hook at low speed for **10 minutes.** Then, add the salt and olive oil, then knead at a higher speed for **3–5 minutes**.
   Dough weight: approx. 445 g
   Dough temperature after kneading: approx. 75–79 °F (24–26 °C)

DAY 1
2:00 PM
Prepare sourdough

7:00 PM
Mix the fermentolyse dough

7:30 PM
Prepare the main dough

9:00 PM
Stretch and fold + put in the refrigerator

DAY 3
3:00 PM
Remove from fridge + shape and final proof

70 ARTISAN SOURDOUGH: BREAD AND BEYOND

ADDITIONAL ITEMS

Neutral vegetable oil for the bowl/container

15 g olive oil

FOR THE TOPPING

90 g grated Gouda

150 g tomato sauce

90 g grated mozzarella

8 slices salami

Fresh basil leaves for sprinkling

Bulk fermentation

4. Let the dough rest, covered, in a lightly oiled bowl or container at room temperature for about **1 hour**. Then stretch and fold the dough before placing it in the refrigerator to ferment at 41–43 °F (5–6 °C) for **24–48 hours**.

Shaping and final proof

5. On the day of baking, pour the olive oil into an oven-proof pan, preferably made of cast iron (10 inches [26 cm] diameter, about 9 inches [23 cm] diameter at the bottom) and thoroughly grease the bottom and sides of the pan with it. Carefully turn the dough out of the bowl or dough tray into the pan and gently turn it once so that the entire dough is coated with olive oil. Using your fingertips, gently press into the dough and stretch it to the edges of the pan. Cover and let the dough rise at room temperature for about **3 hours**.

6. After the dough has proofed, evenly distribute the Gouda over the entire dough, reaching the edges. Spread the tomato sauce over the Gouda, leaving a ½ inch (2 cm) border. Finally, sprinkle the mozzarella on top and cover with the salami.

Baking

7. Preheat the oven to **446 °F (230 °C)** top/bottom heat well in advance. Bake the pizza in the lower third of the oven at **446 °F (230 °C)** for **25–30 minutes**. Then quickly remove from the pan so that the pizza stays crispy and serve sprinkled with fresh basil.

5:30 PM
Preheat oven

6:00 PM
Top and bake

6:30 PM
Remove from the oven

Makes 4 Flatbread Boats | Lievito Madre

KIYMALI PIDE

Pide are stuffed flabread boats—here in a vegetarian version with spinach and Turkish-style white cheese. (See picture on page 74.)

TOTAL TIME	PREPARATION TIME	FERMENTATION TIME	BAKING TIME
6.5–9 hours	1 hour	2–4 hours (sourdough) + 3.5–4 hours (total dough)	15–20 minutes

FOR THE LIEVITO MADRE

60 g Lievito Madre starter
30 g warm water (104°F [40°C])
60 g Type-550 wheat flour

FOR THE DOUGH

3 g fresh yeast (optional)
5 g liquid honey
150 g cool water
60 g whole milk yogurt
Mature Lievito Madre
300 g Type-550 wheat flour
10 g salt
20 g olive oil

ADDITIONAL ITEMS

Neutral vegetable oil for the bowl
Flour for working

1. Whisk the Lievito Madre starter with the warm water until frothy. Then knead thoroughly with the flour. Cover the Lievito Madre and allow it to ferment at 79–86 °F (26–30 °C) for **2–4 hours** until it has doubled in size.

2. For the dough, dissolve the fresh yeast and the honey in the water. Add the whole milk yogurt, Lievito Madre, and wheat flour, then knead with a stand mixer on low speed for **8–10 minutes**. Add the salt and olive oil, then knead at a higher speed for **3–5 minutes**.
   Dough weight: approx. 700 g
   Dough temperature after kneading: approx. 75–79 °F (24–26 °C)

Final proof

3. Let the dough rise, covered, in a lightly oiled bowl at room temperature for **2.5–3 hours** until doubled, stretching and folding after **1 hour** and again after **2 hours**.

ON BAKING DAY

11.00 AM — *Prepare Lievito Madre*
1:00 PM — *Prepare the main dough*
2:20 PM — *Stretch and fold*
3:20 PM — *Stretch and fold + prepare filling*
4:20 PM — *Shape + fill*

ARTISAN SOURDOUGH: BREAD AND BEYOND

FOR THE FILLING

450 g frozen leaf spinach, thawed

1 white onion

1 garlic clove

10 g olive oil

1 tsp. freshly squeezed lemon juice

¼ tsp. salt

2 pinches freshly ground black pepper

1 pinch grated nutmeg

250 g Beyaz peynir (Turkish white cheese) or feta

FOR THE EGG WASH AND TOPPING

1 egg

10 g whole milk

1 pinch salt

1 pinch sugar

White sesame seeds for sprinkling

Black cumin seeds or

Black sesame seeds for sprinkling

4. Prepare the filling while the dough is fermenting. To do this, drain the leaf spinach and squeeze it lightly. Peel the onion and garlic. Finely dice the onion and finely chop the garlic.

5. Heat the olive oil in a pan and sauté the diced onion and chopped garlic until golden brown. Then add the spinach and sauté at medium heat for about **5 minutes**. Finally, season with lemon juice, salt, pepper, and nutmeg. Set the mixture aside and allow it to cool until you are ready to fill the dough.

Shaping and filling

6. Divide the dough into four pieces of about 175 g each. Form the pieces loosely into round balls on a lightly floured work surface, cover, and leave to rest for **15 minutes**. Then carefully roll out into long flatbreads measuring approximately 12 x 6 inches (30 x 15 cm).

7. Mash the white cheese with a fork and mix it with the spinach filling. Spread the filling over the rolled-out dough, leaving a ½ inch (2 cm) border around the edges. Fold the edges inward, pressing and twisting the ends to seal. Place the pide on a baking tray lined with baking paper.

8. For the egg wash, whisk together the egg, whole milk, salt, and sugar, then brush it over the dough edges.

Bulk fermentation

9. Cover the pide loosely and leave to rise at room temperature for about **1 hour**. Then, brush again with the egg wash and sprinkle with sesame and black cumin seeds.

Bake

10. Preheat the oven to 428 °F (220 °C) top/bottom heat well in advance. Bake the pide in the lower third of the oven at 428 °F (220 °C) for about **15–20 minutes**. Then serve while still warm.

4:50 PM
Final proof

5:30 PM
Preheat oven

5:50 PM
Bake

6:10 PM
Remove from the oven

Kiymali Pide (page 72).

Alsatian-Style Beer Cream Flatbread (page 76).

Makes 4 Flatbreads | Lievito Madre

ALSATIAN-STYLE BEER CREAM FLATBREAD

These rustic and delicious flatbreads with a hearty topping are made using a long cold fermentation process. (See picture on page 75.)

TOTAL TIME	PREPARATION TIME	FERMENTATION TIME	TIME ON BAKING DAY
42.5–56.5 hours	50 minutes	2–4 hours (sourdough) + 40–52 hours (total dough)	2.5 hours

FOR THE LIEVITO MADRE
40 g Lievito Madre starter
20 g warm water (104°F [40°C])
40 g Type-550 wheat flour

FOR THE AUTOLYSE DOUGH
200 g non-alcoholic wheat beer
120 g cool water
300 g Type-550 wheat flour
140 g Type-1050 wheat flour

FOR THE MAIN DOUGH
Mature Lievito Madre
5 g beet syrup
0.5 g fresh yeast (optional)
Autolyse dough
10 g salt

1. Whisk the Lievito Madre starter with the warm water until frothy. Then knead with the flour and leave to ferment covered at 79–86 °F (26–30 °C) for **2–4 hours** until well doubled.

2. For the autolyse dough, mix the ingredients briefly but thoroughly and let them rest, covered, for **30–40 minutes**.

3. For the main dough, add the ripe Lievito Madre, beet syrup, and optional fresh yeast to the autolyse dough. Knead the mixture in a stand mixer on low speed for **8–10 minutes**. Then add the salt and knead at a higher speed for **3–5 minutes**.
   Dough weight: approx. 870 g
   Dough temperature after kneading: approx. 75–79 °F (24–26 °C)

DAY 1
4:00 PM — *Prepare Lievito Madre*
5:30 PM — *Mix the autolyse dough*
6:00 PM — *Prepare the main dough*
7:20 PM — *Stretch and fold*
8:20 PM — *Shape into round balls*
8:30 PM — *Put in the refrigerator*

ARTISAN SOURDOUGH: BREAD AND BEYOND

ADDITIONAL ITEMS

Neutral vegetable oil for the bowl/container

Flour for working

FOR THE TOPPING

200 g sour cream

½ tsp. salt

2 pinches freshly ground black pepper

1 pinch grated nutmeg

2 scallions

200 g smoked bacon, diced chives for serving (optional)

Bulk fermentation and ball proofing

4. Place the dough in a lightly oiled bowl or container and let it ferment at room temperature for **2 hours**, stretching and folding it after **1 hour**.

5. Then divide the dough on a lightly floured surface into four pieces of about 215–220 g each and shape them into rounds. Place the dough balls into a greased container or a lightly oiled round bowl. Cover and leave to ferment in the fridge at 43–46 °F (6–8 °C) for **36–48 hours**.

Shaping and final proof

6. On a lightly floured surface, gently pre-shape the dough balls into oval flatbreads and place two on a sheet of parchment paper or a reusable baking liner. Cover and let them proof at room temperature for **2 hours**. Then carefully roll out into long flatbreads measuring 8–10 inches (20–25 cm) in length.

7. For the topping, mix the sour cream with the salt, pepper, and nutmeg. Wash, trim, and finely slice the scallions. Spread the sour cream mixture onto the flatbreads, leaving about a ½ inch (2 cm) border. Sprinkle the diced bacon over the sour cream, followed by the scallions.

Baking

8. Preheat the oven to 482–536 °F (250–280 °C) top/bottom heat well in advance, (the hotter, the better).
   Place the topped flatbreads into the oven and bake them on the second rack from the top for about **6–10 minutes**, keeping an eye on them. Serve immediately, sprinkled with chives if desired.

DAY 3

4:30 PM — *Preforming + final proof*

6:00 PM — *Preheat oven*

6:30 PM — *Top + bake*

6:40 PM — *Remove from the oven*

Makes 2 Large Tarts | Wheat Starter

TARTE FLAMBÉE

This crispy tarte flambée with a thin base is topped with a wonderfully fruity and savory topping.

TOTAL TIME	PREPARATION TIME	RESTING TIME	BAKING TIME
1–1.5 hours	20 minutes	30–60 minutes	10–15 minutes

FOR THE DOUGH
- 120 g wheat starter
- 90 g cool water
- 240 g Type-550 wheat flour + more for working
- 20 g canola oil or olive oil
- 5 g salt

FOR THE TOPPING
- 200 g sour cream or fresh cream
- ¼ tsp. salt
- 2 pinches freshly ground black pepper
- 1 pinch grated nutmeg
- 200 g soft goat cheese (roll)
- 4 fresh figs
- 50 g walnut kernels
- 2 sprigs thyme, leaves picked
- 2 tsp. liquid honey

1. Knead all ingredients together into a smooth dough. Halve it and shape each half of the dough into a round shape. Cover and let rest at room temperature for **30–60 minutes**. Preheat the oven to 536–572 °F (280–300 °C) (as hot as possible) top/bottom heat.

2. After the resting time, roll out the dough thinly on a lightly floured work surface and place it on baking paper. If the dough keeps shrinking a little when rolling it out, let it rest for **10–15 minutes**.

3. For the topping, mix the sour cream with salt, pepper, and nutmeg. Spread the mixture onto the dough, leaving a ½ inch (2 cm) border. Cut the soft goat cheese and figs into thin slices and spread on the sour cream. Roughly chop the walnuts and sprinkle with the thyme.

Baking

4. Bake the tart in the lower third of the oven for about **10–15 minutes** (the baking time may vary depending on the oven and temperature). The dough base should be crispy at the end. Then drizzle the tart with honey and serve immediately.

TIP
Instead of 120 g wheat starter, you can also use Lievito Madre starter.

Makes 1 Onion Tart (springfrom pan, 10 inches [26 cm] diameter) | Rye Starter

ONION TART

This savory and hearty tart, packed with onions and bacon, is a popular pairing with a glass of Federweisser or white wine, especially in wine regions.

TOTAL TIME	PREPARATION TIME	FERMENTATION TIME	BAKING TIME
5.5–8 hours	1 hour	2–4 hours	35 minutes

FOR THE RYE SOURDOUGH
35 g rye starter
35 g warm water (104°F [40°C])
35 g whole rye flour

FOR THE MAIN DOUGH
2 g fresh yeast
100–120 g cold whole milk
Mature rye sourdough
200 g Type-550 wheat flour
5 g salt
10 g lard or butter

ADDITIONAL ITEMS
Neutral vegetable oil for the bowl
Flour for working

1. Mix the rye starter, water, and wholemeal rye flour thoroughly. Let the rye sourdough ferment at 79–82 °F (26–28 °C) for **2–4 hours** until it has doubled in size.

2. For the main dough, dissolve the fresh yeast in the whole milk. Then, using a stand mixer or kneading machine, mix it with the mature rye sourdough and wheat flour at a low speed for **8–10 minutes**. Add the salt and lard, then knead at a higher speed for another **3–5 minutes**.
   Dough weight: approx. 430 g
   Dough temperature after kneading: approx. 75–79 °F (24–26 °C)

Bulk fermentation

3. Let the dough rise in a lightly oiled bowl, covered, at room temperature for **2–2.5 hours** until doubled in size.

Shaping and final proof

4. Line the bottom of a springform pan with parchment paper and lightly grease the sides. Spread the dough into the springform pan and pull up the edges to about 1 inch (3 cm). The dough can be carefully rolled out on a lightly floured work surface or spread out in the pan with your hands and pressed down firmly. Cover and let proof at room temperature for **1 hour**.
Preheat the oven to 250 °F (180 °C) top/bottom heat well in advance.

FOR THE TOPPING

250 g red onions

250 g white onions

100 g smoked bacon, diced

30 g butter

80 g sweet cream

2 medium eggs

40 g rye starter

½ tsp. salt

½ tsp. caraway seeds (optional)

2 pinches freshly ground black pepper

1 pinch grated nutmeg

5. For the topping, peel the red and white onions, cut into thin rings, and set aside.

6. Heat a pan and fry the smoked bacon in it. Add the butter and onion rings and sauté the rings until golden brown. Then let everything cool down for a few minutes.

7. Mix the cream, eggs, rye starter, and salt as well as the caraway seeds, pepper, and grated nutmeg thoroughly. Then mix the mixture into the onion and smoked bacon mixture. Finally, spread the topping on the finished dough base.

Baking

8. Bake the onion tart in the lower third of the preheated oven at 250 °F (180 °C) (top and bottom heat) for about **35 minutes**. Then serve warm.

Makes 1 Tart (springform pan 10 inches [26 cm] diameter). | Lievito Madre

SALMON-SPINACH TART

A savory tart: with a shortcrust pastry base and a creamy filling with smoked salmon and leaf spinach.

TOTAL TIME	PREPARATION TIME	RESTING TIME	BAKING TIME
1.5 hours	20 minutes	30 minutes	15 + 35–40 minutes

FOR THE DOUGH
160 g Type-405 wheat flour
90 g Lievito Madre starter
120 g cold butter
1 egg yolk
½ tsp. salt
Freshly ground black pepper

ADDITIONAL ITEMS
Flour for working
Ceramic baking pearls or dried pulses for blind baking

FOR THE FILLING
1 shallot
20 g butter
300 g fresh leaf spinach
200 g smoked salmon
250 g fresh cream
2 medium eggs
1 egg white
1 garlic clove
½ tsp. salt
2 pinches freshly ground black pepper
Zest from an untreated lemon
1 pinch grated nutmeg
1 Tbsp. chopped flat-leaf parsley

1. For the dough, mix all the ingredients quickly with your hands or briefly in a mixer to form a crumbly dough. Chill in the refrigerator for at least **30 minutes**. Preheat the oven to 250 °F (180 °C) top/bottom heat.

2. After the resting time, roll out the dough on a lightly floured surface. Line a tart or springform pan with the dough, pressing it up the sides to form a 1 ½ inch (4 cm) edge. Prick the dough base with a fork. For blind baking, line the dough with baking paper and fill to the edge with baking pearls. Bake in the middle rack of the oven at 250 °F (180 °C) (top and bottom heat) for about **15 minutes**. Then let it cool down a little. Remove the baking pearls.

3. For the filling, peel and finely dice the shallot. Melt the butter in a pan and sauté the shallots until translucent. Wash and dry the spinach, then add it to the pan and sauté until wilted. Spread the spinach mixture and smoked salmon evenly over the pre-baked tart base.

4. Mix the fresh cream, eggs, and egg whites thoroughly. Peel the garlic and press it. Stir in salt, pepper, lemon zest, nutmeg, and parsley. Carefully pour the mixture over the spinach and smoked salmon.

Baking

5. Bake the tart in the lower third of the preheated oven for about **35–40 minutes** at 250 °F (180 °C) top/bottom heat, until the egg mixture has set. Then serve the tart warm.

Makes 1 Quiche (springform pan 10 inches [26 cm] diameter) | Wheat starter

QUICHE LORRAINE

This savory tart features a shortcrust pastry base and a creamy filling with smoked bacon and flavorful cheese.

TOTAL TIME	PREPARATION TIME	RESTING TIME	BAKING TIME
1.5 hours	20 minutes	30 minutes	15 + 40–50 minutes

FOR THE DOUGH
200 g Type-405 wheat flour
100 g wheat starter
125 g cold butter
1 egg yolk
½ tsp. salt
¼ tsp. freshly ground black pepper

ADDITIONAL ITEMS
Flour for working
Ceramic baking pearls or dried pulses for blind baking

FOR THE FILLING
200 g smoked bacon, diced
100 g Gruyère
200 g whole milk
200 g fresh cream
4 medium eggs
1 egg white
¼ tsp. salt
¼ tsp. freshly ground black pepper
1 pinch grated nutmeg

1. Quickly mix all the dough ingredients by hand or briefly in a food processor until crumbly. Chill in the refrigerator for at least **30 minutes**. Preheat the oven to 250 °F (180 °C) top/bottom heat.

2. After the resting time, roll out the dough on a lightly floured surface. Line a tart or springform pan with the dough, pressing it up the sides to form a 1 ½ inch (4 cm) edge. Prick the dough base with a fork. For blind baking, line the dough with baking paper and fill to the edge with baking pearls.

3. Bake in the lower third of the preheated oven at 250 °F (180 °C) (top and bottom heat) for about **15 minutes**. Then let it cool down a little. Remove the baking pearls.

4. For the filling, fry the smoked bacon in a pan without fat. Then spread evenly on the pre-baked quiche base. Grate the Gruyère and spread it on top.
   Whisk together the whole milk, fresh cream, eggs, and egg white. Stir in the salt, pepper, and nutmeg. Carefully pour the mixture over the bacon and cheese.

   Baking

5. Bake the quiche in the lower third of the preheated oven at 250 °F (180 °C) (top and bottom heat) for about **40–50 minutes**, until the egg mixture is set. Then serve the quiche warm or cold.

> **TIP**
> If you like, you can replace 50 g of the milk for the filling with dry white wine.

Makes 1 Galette | Lievito Madre

MEDITERRANEAN TOMATO GALETTE

This tart-like, savory pie is baked without a pan. The filling consists of creamy herb cream cheese as well as fruity-aromatic tomatoes and spicy feta.

TOTAL TIME	PREPARATION TIME	RESTING TIME	BAKING TIME
80 minutes	20 minutes	30 minutes	30 minutes

FOR THE DOUGH
150 g Lievito Madre starter
50 g olive oil
1 medium egg
120 g Type-550 wheat flour
½ tsp. salt
½ tsp. shredded dried oregano

FOR THE FILLING
100 g herb cream cheese (double cream level)
600 g cherry tomatoes
2 pinches salt
2 pinches freshly ground black pepper
100 g feta
30 g pine nuts
½ tsp. dried oregano

ADDITIONAL ITEMS
Olive oil for brushing
Fresh basil leaves for sprinkling

1. For the dough, quickly knead all ingredients into a compact and smooth dough. Chill in the refrigerator for at least **30 minutes**. Preheat the oven to 392 °F (200 °C) hot air/convection.

2. After chilling, roll out the dough between two sheets of baking paper into a round shape, about 12 inches (30 cm) in diameter.

3. For the filling, spread the cream cheese onto the dough, leaving a border of about ½ inch (2 cm). Wash the cherry tomatoes, halve them, and place them on the cream cheese with the cut side facing up. Season with salt and pepper, then crumble the feta over it. Finally, sprinkle the pine nuts and oregano on top.

4. Fold the exposed dough border over the filling all around. Then brush the dough lightly with olive oil.

Baking

5. Bake the galette in the lower third of the preheated oven at 392 °F (200 °C) convection for about **30 minutes**, until golden brown. Then let it rest for about **10 minutes** and serve sprinkled with basil.

BREAD & ROLLS

Makes 1 Loaf (2 lb. [1 kg] proofing basket) | Rye Starter, Wheat Starter, Lievito Madre

REFRESHING BREAD FOR SOURDOUGH LEFTOVERS

A basic recipe for a mixed bread to use up sourdough leftovers from the fridge: it results in a simple and flavorful everyday bread! (See picture on page 90.)

TOTAL TIME	PREPARATION TIME	FERMENTATION TIME	TIME ON BAKING DAY
6.5–7.5 hours	40 minutes	4.5–5.5 hours (total dough)	6.5–7.5 hours

FOR THE FERMENTOLYSE DOUGH

270 g cool water
150 g sourdough starter (wheat/rye) or
120 g Lievito Madre starter
30 g water
350 g Type-1050 wheat flour
75 g spelt whole grain flour

FOR THE MAIN DOUGH

2–3 g fresh yeast (amount depending on the age and activity of the starter)
10 g beet syrup
Fermentolyse dough
12 g salt
10 g olive oil
20 g water (as needed)

1. For the fermentolyse dough, mix all ingredients briefly but thoroughly and let rest covered for **30 minutes**.

2. For the main dough, add the fresh yeast and syrup to the fermentolyse dough and knead with a stand mixer at low speed for **10 minutes**. Then add the salt and knead at a higher speed for **3–5 minutes**, adding the olive oil in portions and kneading it in. Add up to 20 g of water as needed.
   Dough weight: approx. 900 g
   Dough temperature after kneading: approx. 75–79 °F (24–26 °C)

ON BAKING DAY

- **8:00 AM** Mix the fermentolyse dough
- **8:30 AM** Prepare the main dough
- **9:50 AM** Stretch and fold
- **10:50 AM** Stretch and fold
- **12:20 PM** Shaping + final proof
- **1:20 PM** Preheat oven

ADDITIONAL ITEMS

Neutral vegetable oil for the bowl/container

Flour for working

Bulk fermentation

3. Let the dough rest covered in a lightly oiled bowl or container at room temperature for about **3–4 hours** until doubled in size, stretching and folding after **1 hour and 2 hours**.

Shaping

4. Shape the dough into a round loaf on a floured work surface and place it with the seam side down into a floured proofing basket.

Final proof

5. Cover the dough and allow it to rise at room temperature for about **1.5 hours** until almost ready (see page 30).

Baking

6. Preheat the oven to 464 °F (240 °C) top/bottom heat well in advance.
   Turn the dough out of the proofing basket onto a baking sheet (seam side now up), score it, and immediately add steam (see page 31). Bake for a total of **50 minutes**, releasing the steam after **10 minutes** and reducing the temperature to 410 °F (210 °C). After baking, let the bread cool on a rack and then serve.

1:50 PM
Bake

2:40 PM
Remove from the oven

Refreshing Bread for Sourdough Leftovers (page 90).

Porridge Spelt Bread (page 94).

Makes 1 Loaf (2 lb. [1 kg] proofing basket) | Spelt Starter, Wheat Starter, Lievito Madre

PORRIDGE SPELT BREAD

This succulent spelt bread is made with fermented porridge and a long fermentation in the refrigerator. (See picture on page 93.)

TOTAL TIME	PREPARATION TIME	FERMENTATION TIME	TIME ON BAKING DAY
23–30 hours	50 minutes	4–6 hours (porridge) + 16–21 hours (total dough)	1 hour

FOR THE FERMENTED PORRIDGE

50 g fine spelt or oat flakes
200 g water
10 g sourdough starter (spelt, wheat, or Lievito Madre starter)

FOR THE FERMENTOLYSE DOUGH

Fermented porridge
130 g cold water (41 °F [5 °C])
20 g orange juice
400 g Type-630 spelt flour
100 g spelt whole grain flour

1. For the fermented porridge, toast the spelt flakes in a pan. Add the water, stir, and bring to the boil. Simmer gently at low heat for a few minutes, stirring regularly.

2. Transfer the mixture and allow it to cool to about 86 °F (30 °C). Mix in the sourdough starter and let the porridge ferment at 86 °F (30 °C) for about **4–6 hours**. It is ready when it is filled with bubbles and has slightly increased in volume.

3. Mix all the ingredients briefly but thoroughly and let rest covered at room temperature for **20 minutes**.

THE DAY BEFORE

- 8:00 AM — Cook porridge
- 9:00 AM — Mix sourdough starter with porridge
- 2:00 PM — Mix the fermentolyse dough
- 2:20 PM — Prepare the main dough
- 3.40 PM — Stretch and fold
- 6:40 PM — Shaping + final proof

94 ARTISAN SOURDOUGH: BREAD AND BEYOND

FOR THE MAIN DOUGH

Fermentolyse dough
1 g fresh yeast (optional)
10 g liquid honey
12 g salt
10 g olive oil
30 g water (as needed)

ADDITIONAL ITEMS

Neutral vegetable oil for the bowl/container
Flour for working
Soft spelt or oat flakes

4. For the main dough, knead the fermentolyse dough, fresh yeast, and honey with a stand mixer at low speed for **8–10 minutes**. Then knead at a higher setting for **1–2 minutes**, adding the salt, olive oil, and up to 30 g of water if necessary.
   Dough weight: approx. 950 g
   Dough temperature after kneading: approx. 72–75 °F (22–24 °C)

Bulk fermentation

5. Let the dough rest covered in a lightly oiled bowl or container at 72–75 °F (22–24 °C) for **4–5 hours** until it doubles in size, stretching and folding after **1 hour**.

Shaping

6. Form the dough into a round loaf on a lightly floured work surface. Moisten the smooth side of the dough slightly and roll it in soft spelt flakes. Place the dough, seam side up, in a round proofing basket (it's best to line the basket with a linen cloth).

Final proof

7. Let the dough rest at room temperature for about **30 minutes**, then refrigerate at 41–43 °F (5–6 °C) for **12–16 hours**. The volume should visibly increase.

Baking

8. Preheat the oven to 464 °F (240 °C) top/bottom heat well in advance.
   Turn the dough out of the proofing basket onto a baking sheet (seam side now down), score it, and immediately add steam (see page 31). Steam immediately. Bake the bread for a total of **40–50 minutes**, releasing the steam after **10 minutes** and reducing the temperature to 392 °F (200 °C).
   After baking, let the bread cool on a rack and then serve.

7.10 PM
Put in the refrigerator

ON BAKING DAY
9:00 AM
Preheat oven

9:30 AM
Bake

10:15 AM
Remove from the oven

PORRIDGE SPELT BREAD

Makes 1 Loaf (proofing basket) | Rye Starter

RUSTIC BEER CRUST

This beer crust is a strong and aromatic mixed bread with non-alcoholic wheat beer, made with a two-stage sourdough process. (See picture on page 96.)

TOTAL TIME	PREPARATION TIME	FERMENTATION TIME	TIME ON BAKING DAY
18.5–23 hours	50 minutes	12–15 hours (sourdough, total) + 4.5–6 hours (total dough)	8.5–11 hours

FOR THE SOURDOUGH STAGE 1
5 g rye starter
50 g warm water (104°F [40°C])
50 g Type-1150 rye flour

FOR THE SOURDOUGH STAGE 2
100 g warm water (104°F [40°C])
Entire sourdough from stage 1
100 g whole rye flour

FOR THE FERMENTOLYSE DOUGH
250 g non-alcoholic wheat beer
Mature sourdough from stage 2
300 g Type-550 wheat flour
100 g whole wheat flour
20 g stale bread, toasted and ground

1. For the sourdough stage 1, mix everything thoroughly and let it ferment covered at room temperature for **10–12 hours**.

2. For the sourdough stage 2, mix everything thoroughly and let it ferment covered at 79–82 °F (26–28 °C) for **2–3 hours**.

3. For the fermentolyse dough, mix all the ingredients briefly but thoroughly and let them rest, covered, for **20–30 minutes**.

THE DAY BEFORE
9:00 PM
Sourdough stage 1

ON BAKING DAY
8:00 AM
Sourdough stage 2

10.00 AM
Mix the fermentolyse dough

10.30 AM
Prepare the main dough

11.50 AM
Stretch and fold

2:20 PM
Shaping + final proof

96 ARTISAN SOURDOUGH: BREAD AND BEYOND

FOR THE MAIN DOUGH

10 g beet syrup

Fermentolyse dough

12 g salt

30 g non-alcoholic wheat beer (as needed)

ADDITIONAL ITEMS

Neutral vegetable oil for the bowl/container

Flour for working

4. For the main dough, add the beet syrup to the fermentolyse dough and knead with a stand mixer at low speed for **8–10 minutes**. Add the salt and knead the dough at a higher speed for **3–5 minutes**. Add up to 30 g of non-alcoholic wheat beer as needed.

   Dough weight: approx. 1,020 g

   Dough temperature after kneading: approx. 75–79 °F (24–26 °C)

Bulk fermentation

5. Let the dough rise covered in a lightly oiled bowl or container at 71–75 °F (22–24 °C) for about **3–4 hours** until it doubles in size, stretching and folding after **1 hour**.

Shaping

6. Shape the dough into a round loaf on a floured work surface and place it with the seam side down into a floured proofing basket.

Final proof

7. Let the dough rise covered at 71–75 °F (22–24 °C) for about **1.5–2 hours** until it is almost fully proofed (see page 30).

Baking

8. Preheat the oven to 482 °F (250 °C) top/bottom heat well in advance.
   Turn the dough out of the proofing basket onto a baking sheet (seam side up), score it, and immediately add steam (see page 31). Bake for a total of **50 minutes**, releasing the steam after **10 minutes** and reducing the temperature to 410 °F (210 °C). After baking, let the beer crust cool on a rack, then serve.

3:30 PM
Preheat oven

4:00 PM
Bake

4:50 PM
Remove from the oven

RUSTIC BEER CRUST

Rustic Beer Crust (page 96).

Country Loaf (page 100).

Makes 1 Loaf (2 lb. [1 kg] loaf tin) | Rye Starter

COUNTRY LOAF

A recipe for an aromatic and simple wheat-rye mixed bread from a loaf pan with a two-stage rye sourdough. (See picture on page 99.)

TOTAL TIME	PREPARATION TIME	FERMENTATION TIME	TIME ON BAKING DAY
16.5–20 hours	40 minutes	12–15 hours (sourdough, total) + 3–3.5 hours (total dough)	6.5–8 hours

FOR THE SOURDOUGH STAGE 1
8 g rye starter
80 g warm water (104°F [40°C])
80 g Type-1150 rye flour

FOR THE SOURDOUGH STAGE 2
Entire sourdough from stage 1
160 g warm water (104°F [40°C])
160 g Type-1150 rye flour

FOR THE FERMENTOLYSE DOUGH
200 g warm water (104°F [40°C])
Mature sourdough from stage 2
340 g Type-1050 wheat flour

1. For the sourdough stage 1, mix everything thoroughly and let it ferment covered at room temperature for **10–12 hours**.

2. For the sourdough stage 2, mix everything thoroughly and let it ferment covered at 79–82 °F (26–28 °C) for **2–3 hours**.

3. For the fermentolyse dough, mix all the ingredients briefly but thoroughly and let rest covered at room temperature for **30 minutes**.

THE DAY BEFORE
9:00 PM
Sourdough stage 1

ON BAKING DAY
8:00 AM
Sourdough stage 2

10.00 AM
Mix the fermentolyse dough

10.30 AM
Prepare the main dough

10.40 AM
Proofing

11.00 AM
Shaping

ARTISAN SOURDOUGH: BREAD AND BEYOND

FOR THE MAIN DOUGH

10 g liquid wild honey
(alternative beet syrup)
14 g salt
Fermentolyse dough

ADDITIONAL ITEMS

Neutral vegetable oil for greasing the pan (optional)
Rye flour for sprinkling
Flour for working

4. For the main dough, add the honey and salt to the fermentolyse dough. Mix with a food processor/kneading machine on low speed for **5–8 minutes** until you have a soft and sticky dough. (Can also be done by hand.)

   Dough weight: approx. 1,050 g
   Dough temperature after kneading: approx. 79–82 °F (26–28 °C)

Bulk fermentation (bread-tin proofing)

5. Let the dough rest covered in the mixing bowl at room temperature for about **20 minutes**.

Shaping

6. Either grease a loaf tin and sprinkle with rye flour or line with baking foil. Shape the dough on a well-floured work surface into an elongated loaf and place it seam-side down in the loaf pan. Alternatively, fill the dough directly into the loaf pan and smooth it with a damp dough scraper. Then sprinkle with rye flour.

Final proof

7. Let the dough proof covered at 77–81 °F (25–27 °C) for about **2.5–3 hours** (or alternatively at 72–75 °F (22–24 °C) for about **5 hours**), uncovering it halfway through the proofing time to promote cracks on the dough surface. The dough should rise to about the edge of the 2 lb. (1 kg) loaf pan.

Baking

8. Preheat the oven to 464 °F (240 °C) top/bottom heat well in advance.
   Put the bread in the oven and immediately add a little steam. Bake for a total of **50 minutes**, reducing the temperature to 410 °F (210 °C) after **5 minutes** and letting the steam escape.

9. Immediately after baking, remove the bread from the loaf pan, spray with a little water and let it cool on a rack. Then serve the bread.

1:30 PM
Preheat oven

2:00 PM
Bake

2:50 PM
Remove from the oven

COUNTRY LOAF

Makes 1 Loaf (2 lb. [1 kg] loaf tin) | Rye Starter

WHOLEMEAL RYE AND SPELT BREAD

A recipe for a succulent full-grain bread baked in a loaf pan with rye and spelt whole grain flour, rye meal, and seeds. (See picture on page 102.)

TOTAL TIME	PREPARATION TIME	FERMENTATION TIME	TIME ON BAKING DAY
15–17 hours	50 minutes	10–12 hours (sourdough) + 3 hours (dough)	5 hours

FOR THE SOURDOUGH

10 g rye starter
120 g warm water (104°F [40°C])
120 g whole rye flour

FOR THE SOAKING MIXTURE

60 g stale bread, toasted and ground
5 g salt
180 g hot water (194°F [90°C])

FOR THE SWELLING MIXTURE

70 g sunflower seeds, roasted
20 g white sesame seeds, roasted
125 g coarse rye meal
8 g salt
180 g cool water

FOR THE FERMENTOLYSE DOUGH

Prepared sourdough
100 g cool water
250 g spelt whole grain flour

1. For the sourdough, mix everything thoroughly and let it ferment while covered at room temperature for **10–12 hours**.

2. For the soaking mixture, mix everything together, cover, and leave to soak at room temperature overnight (approx. **10–12 hours**).

3. For the swelling mixture, mix everything together, cover, and leave to soak at room temperature overnight (approx. **10–12 hours**).

4. For the fermentolyse dough, mix all ingredients briefly but thoroughly and let rest covered for **20 minutes**.

THE DAY BEFORE
9:00 PM
Prepare sourdough + soak + swell parts

ON BAKING DAY
8:00 AM
Mix the fermentolyse dough

8.20 AM
Prepare the main dough

8.40 AM
Shaping + final proof

11.10 AM
Preheat oven

11.40 AM
Bake

102 | ARTISAN SOURDOUGH: BREAD AND BEYOND

FOR THE MAIN DOUGH

2 g fresh yeast (optional)

20 g beet syrup

Fermentolyse dough

Soaking mix

Swelling mix

ADDITIONAL ITEMS

Neutral vegetable oil for greasing the pan (optional)

Sunflower seeds for sprinkling

White sesame seeds for sprinkling

5. For the main dough, add the fresh yeast and syrup to the fermentolyse dough and knead with a stand mixer at low speed for **5–8 minutes**. Then, increase the speed and knead for another **1–2 minutes**, incorporating the soaking mixture and swelling mixture. Mix everything together into a soft, binding, and slightly sticky dough.

    Dough weight: approx. 1,270 g

    Dough temperature after kneading: 72–75 °F (22–24 °C)

Shaping

6. Grease a loaf pan and either sprinkle it with sunflower seeds and sesame seeds, or line it with nonstick baking paper. Fill the dough into the pan, smooth it with a damp dough scraper, and sprinkle with sunflower seeds and sesame seeds.

Final proof

7. Let the dough rise covered at 72–75 °F (22–24 °C) for about **3 hours**.

It should rise to about ½ inch (2 cm) below the edge of the 2 lb. (1 kg) loaf pan.

Baking

8. Preheat the oven to 446 °F (230 °C) top/bottom heat well in advance.

Put the bread in the oven and immediately add a little steam. Bake for **80 minutes**, releasing the steam after **10 minutes** and reducing the temperature to 392 °F (200 °C).

Immediately after baking, remove the bread from the loaf pan, spray with a little water, and let it cool on a rack. Serve it fresh.

> **TIP**
> For the stale bread, dice it into small pieces and spread it on a baking tray. You can use the residual heat of the oven after baking to toast the cubes. Once the bread cubes are completely dry and cooled, they can be crushed using a mixer or meat grinder.

1:00 PM
Remove from the oven

Wholemeal Rye and Spelt Bread (page 102).

Smoky Almond and Bacon Twisted Rolls (page 106).

Makes 8–10 Rolls | Rye Starter, Wheat Starter

SMOKY ALMOND AND BACON TWISTED ROLLS

This recipe combines mixed sourdough, fried bacon, and smoked almonds to make savory twisted rolls. (See picture on page 105.)

TOTAL TIME	PREPARATION TIME	FERMENTATION TIME	TIME ON BAKING DAY
15–19 hours	40 minutes	10–14 hours (sourdough) + 4 hours (dough, total)	6 hours

FOR THE MIXED SOURDOUGH

10 g rye or wheat starter
150 g warm water (104°F [40°C])
75 g Type-1050 wheat flour
75 g Type-1150 rye flour

FOR THE AUTOLYSE DOUGH

200 g water
350 g Type-550 wheat flour

FOR THE MAIN DOUGH

200 g smoked bacon, diced
100 g smoked almonds
Mixed sourdough
1 g fresh yeast (optional)
5 g beet syrup
Autolyse dough
8 g salt
20 g water (as needed)

1. For the mixed sourdough, mix everything thoroughly and let it ferment covered at room temperature for **3 hours**.

2. For the autolyse dough, briefly but thoroughly mix water and flour, then let it sit covered at room temperature for **40–60 minutes** to hydrate.

3. For the main dough, fry the smoked bacon cubes in a pan and then let them cool. Roughly chop the smoked almonds. Set both aside.

4. Add the mixed sourdough, fresh yeast, and beet syrup to the autolyse dough and knead with a stand mixer at low speed for **8–10 minutes**. Then add the salt and knead on a higher speed for another **3–5 minutes**, adding up to 20 g of water if needed. Then briefly knead in the smoked bacon and smoked almonds by hand.
   Dough weight: approx. 1,190 g
   Dough temperature after kneading: approx. 75–79 °F (24–26 °C)

THE DAY BEFORE
9:30 PM
Prepare sourdough

ON BAKING DAY
8:00 AM
Mix the autolyse dough

8.40 AM
Prepare the main dough

10.00 AM
Stretch and fold

11.00 AM
Stretch and fold

12:00 PM
Shaping + final proof

106 ARTISAN SOURDOUGH: BREAD AND BEYOND

ADDITIONAL ITEMS

Neutral vegetable oil for the bowl/container

Flour for working

Bulk fermentation

5. Let the dough rise covered in a lightly oiled bowl or container at 71–75 °F (22–24 °C) for about **3 hours**, stretching and folding after **1 hour and 2 hours**. (Using a rectangular container, like a dough tub, will help in evenly cutting rectangular dough pieces later.)

Shaping

6. Turn the dough out onto a floured work surface and sprinkle the top thinly with flour. Then use the dough scraper to cut out eight to ten long dough pieces. Carefully twist the dough pieces two or three times. Then, place the dough pieces the other way round (than they will be later baked) into a floured baker's linen or kitchen towel, gently pulling the fabric between the dough pieces to support them.

Final proof

7. Let the rolls rise covered at room temperature for about **1 hour**, until nearly proofed (see page 30).

Baking

8. Preheat the oven to 482 °F (250 °C) top/bottom heat well in advance.
Place the dough pieces on a sheet of baking paper or baking foil on the baking tray the other way around than they are in the baking linen, then place them in the tray and steam them immediately. Bake for a total of **20–25 minutes**, releasing the steam after **10 minutes** and reducing the temperature to 410 °F (210 °C).

9. After baking, spray the rolls with water and let them cool on a rack. Then serve.

12.30 PM
Preheat oven

1:00 PM
Bake

1:25 PM
Remove from the oven

SMOKY ALMOND AND BACON TWISTED ROLLS

Makes 10 Buns | Lievito Madre

OLIVE OIL BRIOCHE BURGER BUNS

These buns are soft hamburger rolls with a fluffy, airy crumb and a rich, aromatic flavor. (See picture on page 110.)

TOTAL TIME	PREPARATION TIME	FERMENTATION TIME	TIME ON BAKING DAY
7.5–10 hours	50 minutes	2–4 hours (sourdough) + 4.5–5 hours (total dough)	7.5–10 hours

FOR THE LIEVITO MADRE

60 g Lievito Madre starter
(it should be very active and the last refresher should have been no more than 12 hours ago)
30 g warm water (104°F [40°C])
60 g Type-550 wheat flour

FOR THE MAIN DOUGH

Mature Lievito Madre
150 g cold whole milk
40 g sugar
3 cold medium eggs
500 g Type-550 wheat flour
10 g salt
90 g mild olive oil
50 g cool water (as needed)

1. Whisk the Lievito Madre starter with the warm water until frothy. Then knead the mixture with the flour. Cover the Lievito Madre and allow it to ferment at 78–86°F (26–30°C) for **2–4 hours** until it has doubled in size.

2. For the main dough, combine all ingredients, except salt, olive oil, and water, in a stand mixer at low speed for about **8–10 minutes**. Then add the salt and continue kneading at low speed for another **10–15 minutes**, adding the olive oil in portions and incorporating it into the dough. Next, knead at high speed for **3–5 minutes** until the dough becomes slightly sticky. Add up to 50 g of water if necessary. (It is better to knead for a shorter time than to over-knead. The dough structure continues to develop during the bulk fermentation.)
   Dough weight: approx. 1,120 g
   Dough temperature after kneading: approx. 75–79°F (24–26°C)

ON BAKING DAY

8:00 AM	10:30 AM	11:45 AM	12:30 PM	2:00 PM	3:30 PM
Prepare Lievito Madre	Prepare the main dough	Stretch and fold	Stretch and fold	Shaping + final proof	Preheat oven

ARTISAN SOURDOUGH: BREAD AND BEYOND

ADDITIONAL ITEMS

Neutral vegetable oil for the bowl/container

Flour for working

FOR THE EGG WASH AND TOPPING

1 egg

10 g whole milk

1 pinch salt

1 pinch sugar

White and black sesame seeds for sprinkling

50 g melted butter to brush

> **TIP**
> The olive oil brioche burger buns are great to bake in advance and freeze.

Bulk fermentation

3. Let the dough rise covered in a lightly oiled bowl or container at 79–81 °F (25–27 °C) for about **3 hours**, until the volume has doubled or, ideally, tripled.

4. Stretch and fold the dough after **45 and 90 minutes**. (The fermentation time may vary depending on the activity of the sourdough.)

Shaping

5. Divide the dough on a floured surface into ten pieces, each weighing about 110 g, and shape them into smooth, round rolls.

Final proof

6. Let the rolls rest covered at room temperature for **1.5–2 hours** until fully proofed (see page 30).

Baking

7. Preheat the oven to 428 °F (220 °C) top/bottom heat well in advance.

8. For the egg wash, whisk together the egg, milk, salt, and sugar. Once the dough pieces are fully proofed, gently flatten them and brush with the egg wash. Then sprinkle with sesame seeds as a topping.

9. Place the dough pieces in the oven and steam them a little. Bake for **16–18 minutes**, reducing the temperature to 356–392 °F (180–200 °C) after **10 minutes**. Do not release the steam throughout the baking process. While baking, melt the butter.

10. After baking, immediately brush the hot burger buns with the melted butter. Allow to cool on a rack, covered with a kitchen towel. Serve them fresh.

4:00 PM
Bake

4:20 PM
Remove from the oven

Olive Oil Brioche Burger Buns (page 108).

Wheat Rolls (page 112).

Makes 9 Rolls | Wheat Starter

WHEAT ROLLS

A recipe for classic white rolls with a crispy crust and a light, aromatic outside. (See picture on page 111.)

TOTAL TIME	PREPARATION TIME	FERMENTATION TIME	TIME ON BAKING DAY
5.5 hours	40 minutes	4 hours (total dough)	5.5 hours

FOR THE FERMENTOLYSE DOUGH
150 g cold whole milk
120 g cool water
100 g cold wheat sourdough starter
450 g Type-550 wheat flour

FOR THE MAIN DOUGH
5 g fresh yeast
10 g liquid honey
Fermentolyse dough
11 g salt
10 g butter
20 g water (as needed)

1. For the fermentolyse dough, mix everything briefly but thoroughly, and let it sit covered at room temperature for **20–30 minutes** to hydrate.

2. For the main dough, add the fresh yeast and honey to the fermentolyse dough and knead with a stand mixer at low speed for **10 minutes**. Then add the salt and butter, and knead at higher speed for **3–5 minutes**, adding up to 20 g of water if necessary.
   Dough weight: approx. 870 g
   Dough temperature after kneading: approx. 75–79 °F (24–26 °C)

ON BAKING DAY

8:00 AM	8:30 AM	9:50 AM	10:50 AM	11.50 AM	12.30 PM
Mix the fermentolyse dough	Prepare the main dough	Stretch and fold	Stretch and fold	Shaping + final proof	Preheat oven

ARTISAN SOURDOUGH: BREAD AND BEYOND

ADDITIONAL ITEMS

Neutral vegetable oil for the bowl/container

Flour for working

Bulk fermentation

3. Let the dough rest covered in a lightly oiled bowl or container at room temperature for about **3 hours** until doubled in size, stretching and folding after **1 hour** and **2 hours**.

Shaping

4. On a floured work surface, divide the dough into nine pieces, each weighing about 95 g. Shape the dough pieces loosely into rounds and let them rest for **15 minutes** with the dough seam facing downwards. Then carefully shape the dough into long pieces. Place the rolls with the seam side up into a lightly floured baker's linen or kitchen towel, slightly raising the fabric between the rolls to support them.

Final proof

5. Let the rolls rise covered at room temperature for about **1 hour**, until nearly proofed (see page 30).

Baking

6. Preheat the oven to 464 °F (240 °C) top/bottom heat well in advance.
   Place the rolls seam side down onto a piece of parchment paper or reusable baking sheet on a baking tray. Using a sharp knife, score the rolls lengthwise, and then bake with steam. Bake for **18–20 minutes**, reducing the temperature to 392 °F (200 °C) after **10 minutes**.

7. Spray the rolls with a little water, let them cool on a rack, and serve.

1:00 PM
Bake

1:20 PM
Remove from the oven

Makes 9–10 Rolls | Rye Starter, Lievito Madre

SPELT AND OAT ROLLS

*Fluffy and airy spelt rolls with oats,
made with overnight fermentation. (See picture on page 116.)*

TOTAL TIME	PREPARATION TIME	FERMENTATION TIME	TIME ON BAKING DAY
13.5–15.5 hours	40 minutes	10.5–12.5 hours (total dough)	1 hour

FOR THE SOURDOUGH COOKING PIECE

50 g rye starter
30 g whole grain oat flakes
160 g water

FOR THE AUTOLYSE DOUGH

180 g cool water
20 g orange juice (natural source of vitamin C, to strengthen the sourdough structure)
Cold sourdough flour dough
300 g Type-630 spelt flour
175 g spelt whole grain flour

FOR THE MAIN DOUGH

10 g honey
1 g fresh yeast
10 g Lievito Madre starter or wheat/spelt starter
Autolyse dough
12 g salt
10 g butter
20 g water (as needed)

1. For the sourdough cooking piece, mix the rye sourdough starter, oats, and water in a pot using a whisk until there are no lumps. Heat slowly and continue stirring. After a few minutes the mixture begins to thicken like pudding. Remove the pot from the heat, transfer the sourdough cook-up to another container, and let it cool for a few minutes. Then cover with cling film and chill in the fridge for at least **2 hours**.

2. For the autolyse dough, mix everything briefly but thoroughly, and let it sit covered at room temperature for **20 minutes** to hydrate.

3. For the main dough, add the honey, fresh yeast, and sourdough starter to the autolyse dough and knead for **8–10 minutes** using a food processor/kneading machine on a low setting. Then increase the speed to medium for another **1–2 minutes**, adding the salt, butter, and up to 20 g of water as needed.
   Dough weight: approx. 970 g
   Dough temperature after kneading: approx. 72–75 °F (22–24 °C)

THE DAY BEFORE
5:00 PM — *Make the rye sourdough starter*
8:00 PM — *Mix autolyse dough*
8:20 PM — *Prepare the main dough*
9:25 PM — *Stretch and fold*
10:10 PM — *Stretch and fold*

ON BAKING DAY
7:30 AM — *Shaping + final proof*

ARTISAN SOURDOUGH: BREAD AND BEYOND

ADDITIONAL ITEMS

Neutral vegetable oil for the bowl/container

Flour for working

FOR THE SOURDOUGH WASH AND TOPPING

30 g rye starter

30 g water

Coarse oat flakes for sprinkling

> **TIP**
>
> For a yeast-free variant, 40 g of refreshed Lievito Madre can be used instead of 10 g of Lievito Madre starter and 1 g of fresh yeast. Allow the dough to ferment at 72–75 °F (22–24 °C) during the bulk fermentation phase.

Bulk fermentation

4. Let the dough rise in a lightly oiled bowl or container at 64–60 °F (18–20 °C) for **10–12 hours** until it has doubled in volume, stretching and folding the dough at **45 and 90 minutes**. (Using a rectangular container, like a dough tub, will help in evenly cutting rectangular dough pieces later.)

Shaping

5. Turn the dough out onto a floured work surface and sprinkle the top thinly with flour. Using a dough cutter, cut the dough into 9–10 rectangular pieces. Place the pieces onto a floured baker's linen or kitchen towel, pulling the fabric between the rolls slightly to help support them.

Final proof

6. Let the rolls rest for **30–40 minutes**, covered. Then transfer them to a piece of parchment paper or reusable baking sheet.

7. For the sourdough wash, mix the rye sourdough starter and water together. Spread the mixture over the dough pieces and then sprinkle with oat flakes as a topping.

Baking

8. Preheat the oven to 464 °F (240 °C) top/bottom heat well in advance.
   Place the rolls in the oven and immediately create steam. Bake for a total of **20–22 minutes**, releasing the steam after **10 minutes** and reducing the temperature to 410 °F (210 °C).

9. Bake the rolls, then allow them to cool on a rack before serving.

7.40 AM
Preheat oven

8:00 AM
Bake

8.20 AM
Remove from the oven

SPELT AND OAT ROLLS

Spelt and Oat Rolls (page 114).

Breadsticks with Parmesan Crust (page 120).

NIBBLES

Makes 20 Breadsticks | Wheat Starter

BREADSTICKS WITH PARMESAN CRUST

A savory snack inspired by the breadsticks from Pizza Hut® restaurants. The breadsticks are perfect for dipping or as a side dish for grilling, salads, or soups. (See picture on page 117.)

TOTAL TIME	PREPARATION TIME	FERMENTATION TIME	BAKING TIME
6.5–9 hours	50 minutes	2–4 hours (sourdough) + 3–3.5 hours (total dough)	12–15 minutes

FOR THE FLOUR DOUGH
125 g water
25 g durum wheat flour (Semola rimacinata)

FOR THE SOURDOUGH
70 g wheat starter
70 g warm water (104°F [40°C])
70 g Type-1050 wheat flour

FOR THE MAIN DOUGH
50–70 g cold water cold flour dough
Mature sourdough
3 g fresh yeast
5 g honey
300 g Type-550 wheat flour
15 g olive oil
8 g salt

1. Whisk the water and flour in a pot until smooth and lump-free. Heat slowly and continue stirring. After a few minutes, the mixture will begin to thicken into a pudding-like consistency. Transfer the mixture to another container and allow it to cool for a few minutes. Then cover the flour dough with plastic wrap and refrigerate for at least **2 hours**.

2. For the sourdough, thoroughly mix the wheat starter with the warm water and flour. Cover the sourdough and allow it to ferment at 78–86 °F (26–30 °C) for **2–4 hours** until it has doubled in size.

3. For the main dough, mix all ingredients except for olive oil and salt with a stand mixer at low speed for **10 minutes**. Start with the smaller amount of water. Then add the olive oil and salt, and knead at higher speed for **5–8 minutes** until you get a smooth dough. Add any remaining water as needed.
   Dough weight: approx. 750 g
   Dough temperature after kneading: approx. 75–79 °F (24–26 °C)

ON BAKING DAY

8:00 AM	8.10 AM	10.30 AM	12:00 PM	1:30 PM	1:40 PM
Prepare flour dough	Prepare sourdough	Prepare the main dough	Stretch and fold	Shaping	Preheat oven

ARTISAN SOURDOUGH: BREAD AND BEYOND

ADDITIONAL ITEMS

Neutral vegetable oil for the bowl/container

Flour (for example durum wheat flour) for working

FOR THE TOPPING

60 g olive oil

2 Tbsp. finely grated Parmesan cheese

2 tsp. breadcrumbs

1 tsp. garlic powder

1 tsp. onion powder

1 tsp. dried oregano

¼ tsp. salt

¼ tsp. chili powder

2 pinches freshly ground black pepper

Bulk fermentation

4. Let the dough rise in a lightly oiled bowl or container, covered, at room temperature for about **2.5–3 hours** until it has doubled in size, stretching and folding the dough after **1 hour**. (Using a rectangular container, like a dough tub, will help in evenly cutting rectangular dough pieces later.)

Shaping

5. Turn the risen dough onto a floured work surface and lightly flour the top. Roll out the dough to about 12 x 12 inches (30 × 30 cm). Then cut out 20 pieces of dough, each about 1 inch (3 cm) wide and 6 inches (15 cm) long. Spread the dough pieces on a baking tray lined with baking paper or baking foil.

Final proof

6. Let the rolls rest for **30–40 minutes**, covered.

7. Mix the ingredients together and spread the topping on the dough pieces after they have risen.

Baking

8. Preheat the oven to 446 °F (230 °C) with convection.

9. Place the breadsticks in the oven and immediately add steam (see page 31). Bake at 446 °F (230 °C) convection for a total of **12–15 minutes**, releasing the steam after **5 minutes**. If the breadsticks brown too much, reduce the temperature to 410 °F (210 °C).

10. After baking, let the breadsticks cool on a rack and then serve.

2:00 PM
Prepare topping + spread on dough pieces

2:10 PM
Bake

2:25 PM
Remove from the oven

Makes 1 Sheet | Rye Starter

PUMPKIN AND CHEESE CRACKERS

These savory, hearty whole grain crackers are easy to make and perfect as a healthy snack or for nibbling in between meals.

TOTAL TIME
4.5–5 hours

PREPARATION TIME
20 minutes

FERMENTATION TIME
3–4 hours

BAKING TIME
60–80 minutes

FOR THE DOUGH

200 g warm water (104°F [40°C])
150 g rye starter
3 g fresh yeast
10 g beet syrup
60 g pumpkin seeds
120 g whole rye flour
50 g rolled oats
25 g ground flaxseed
20 g white sesame seeds, roasted
5 g salt
10 g pumpkin seed oil or olive oil

FOR THE TOPPING

120 g Gouda
Pumpkin seeds for sprinkling

1. For the dough, mix the water, rye starter, fresh yeast, and beet syrup. Coarsely chop the pumpkin seeds. Mix everything thoroughly with the remaining ingredients. Spread the dough as thinly and evenly as possible onto a baking tray lined with baking paper or baking foil. Let it rest uncovered at room temperature for **3–4 hours**.

2. For the topping, grate the cheese.

Baking

3. Preheat the oven to 302°F (150°C) with convection. Bake the crackers at 302°F (150°C) hot air/convection for about **60–80 minutes**: open the oven door occasionally to release excess moisture. After **15 minutes** of baking, cut the dough to the desired size (e.g. using a pizza cutter). After another **15 minutes** (i.e. after **30 minutes** baking time), first sprinkle the grated cheese evenly over the dough as a topping and then the pumpkin seeds.
The crackers are ready when the dough is properly baked and dry. Then let the crackers cool down and either serve immediately or store in an airtight container.

Makes 60 Pieces | Lievito Madre

TARALLI PUGLIESI

Taralli Pugliesi is a savory snack widely popular in southern Italy—crispy, crunchy rings with a Mediterranean flair.

TOTAL TIME	PREPARATION TIME	RESTING TIME	BAKING TIME
8.5–9 hours	1 hour	7–7.5 hours	35–40 minutes

FOR THE DOUGH
- 1 tsp. fennel seeds
- 175–200 g dry white wine
- 75 g Lievito Madre starter
- 450 g Type-550 wheat flour
- 125 g olive oil
- 15 g salt

1. Crush the fennel seeds in a mortar. Knead with the remaining ingredients for **5–8 minutes** into a smooth dough, starting with the lower amount of white wine. Gradually add more wine as needed until a firm and pliable dough forms. Cover and let the dough rest in the refrigerator for **30–60 minutes**. (Dough weight: approx. 840 g)

Shaping

2. Divide the dough into pieces of about 10 g each. Roll each piece of dough into a strand about 4 inches (10 cm) long. Wrap it around two fingers to form a ring. Press the ends together lightly and place the ring on a kitchen towel.

Cook

3. Bring water to the boil in a large pot and then reduce the heat. Add the dough rings in batches and let them simmer in the hot water. As soon as they float to the surface, remove them with a slotted spoon and let them drain on a clean kitchen towel.

Dry

4. Spread the boiled and drained Taralli on two baking sheets lined with parchment paper or a reusable baking sheet. Cover with a kitchen towel. Let dry for at least **6 hours**.

Baking

5. Preheat the oven to 250 °F (180 °C) hot air/convection. Bake the Taralli until golden brown in about **35–40 minutes**. They are ready when the dough is properly baked and dry; this makes the Taralli crumbly and crispy.
Let the Taralli cool and serve immediately or store in an airtight container.

TIP
To vary the taste: replace the fennel seeds with dried anise, rosemary, pepper, garlic, or chili as desired. You can roll the Taralli in white sesame seeds after boiling.

Makes 30 Pieces | Lievito Madre

GRISSINI

Grissini—the crispy, savory snack is a true Italian finger food classic.

TOTAL TIME	PREPARATION TIME	FERMENTATION TIME	TIME ON BAKING DAY
3.5–4 hours	45 minutes	2.5–3 hours (total dough)	3.5–4 hours

FOR THE DOUGH
200 g water
150 g Lievito Madre starter
3 g fresh yeast
200 g Type-550 wheat flour
100 g durum wheat flour (Semola rimacinata)
20 g olive oil
8–10 g salt

ADDITIONAL ITEMS
Neutral vegetable oil for the bowl
Flour for working

1. For the dough, knead all ingredients except olive oil and salt in a stand mixer at low speed for **5–8 minutes**. Then add the olive oil and salt and knead at a higher speed for another **5–8 minutes** until smooth. The dough should be firm but pliable. (Dough weight: approx. 680 g)

Bulk fermentation

2. Let the dough rise in a lightly oiled bowl, covered, at room temperature for **1.5–2 hours** until nearly doubled in volume.

Shaping

3. On a lightly floured work surface, divide the dough into pieces of 20–25 g each (maximum). Roll each piece into a strand about 12 inches (30 cm) long. If the strands shrink back, let them rest for **10–15 minutes** before rolling again.

Final proof

4. Place the strands on two baking sheets lined with parchment paper or a reusable baking sheet. Cover with a kitchen towel and let rise at room temperature for about **1 hour**.

Baking

5. Preheat the oven to 428 °F (220 °C) with convection. (With top/bottom heat, the baking temperature is around 464 °F (240 °C), then bake the trays one after the other.)

6. Bake the grissini at 428 °F (220 °C) hot air/convection for **10–15 minutes**. They are ready when the dough is properly baked and dry; this makes the grissini crumbly and crispy.
Let the grissini cool and serve immediately or store in an airtight container.

ARTISAN SOURDOUGH: BREAD AND BEYOND

Makes 2 Baking Sheets | Wheat Starter

CRISPY CRACKERS

These simple and crispy crackers are perfect for snacking and can be endlessly varied with different toppings.

TOTAL TIME	PREPARATION TIME	RESTING TIME
1–1.5 hours	20 minutes	30–60 minutes

FOR THE DOUGH
225 g Type-550 wheat flour
150 g wheat starter
75 g lukewarm water
25 g olive oil
5 g salt

FOR THE SOURDOUGH GLAZE
30 g wheat starter
20 g water

FOR THE TOPPING
Fleur de Sel for sprinkling
White sesame seeds for sprinkling
Black sesame seeds for sprinkling

VARIATIONS FOR THE TOPPING AS DESIRED
Freshly ground black pepper
1 tsp. dried oregano
1 tsp. chili powder
4 Tbsp. grated Parmesan

1. Knead all ingredients into a smooth dough and let it rest, covered, at room temperature for **30–60 minutes**. Then divide the dough in half and roll each portion as thinly and evenly as possible (about 1 mm thick) on a sheet of parchment paper or a reusable baking sheet. If the dough shrinks back, let it rest for **10–15 minutes** before rolling again.

2. For the sourdough glaze, mix the wheat starter and water thoroughly, then brush the dough thinly with the mixture. Sprinkle with Fleur de Sel and sesame seeds as a topping. Use a pizza cutter to cut the dough into diamonds or squares of about 1 ½ inch (4 cm) in size.

Baking

3. Preheat the oven to 482 °F (250 °C) with convection. Bake the crackers in a preheated oven at 482 °F (250 °C) hot air/convection for about **8–12 minutes**, with sight until crispy. They are done when they are completely dry.
Let the crackers cool and serve immediately or store in an airtight container.

Makes 1 Sheet | Rye Starter

ASIAN-STYLE CRACKERS

These simple and crispy crackers made with spelt flour get their Asian flair from plenty of sesame and soy sauce.

TOTAL TIME
50–80 minutes

PREPARATION TIME
20 minutes

RESTING TIME
30–60 minutes

FOR THE DOUGH
100 g rye starter
50 g spelt whole grain flour
50 g Type-630 spelt flour
15 g toasted sesame oil
20 g soy sauce (Tamari or Shoyu)
25 g white sesame seeds, roasted
5 g black sesame seeds
1 pinch salt

1. Knead all ingredients together into a smooth dough. Cover and let rest at room temperature for **30–60 minutes**. Preheat the oven to 320 °F (160 °C) with convection.

2. After the resting period, roll out the dough as thinly and evenly as possible (about 1 mm thick) on a sheet of parchment paper or a reusable baking sheet. Use a pizza cutter to cut the dough into diamonds or squares of about 1 ½ inch (4 cm) in size.

   Baking
3. Bake the crackers on the lower third rack of the preheated oven at 320 °F (160 °C) convection for about **15 minutes**, keeping an eye on them.
   They are done when they are completely dry.
   Let the crackers cool and serve immediately or store in an airtight container.

SWEET BAKED GOODS

Makes 12 Rolls | Lievito Madre

SWEDISH CINNAMON ROLLS

These yeast-raised buns with a long fermentation time and a buttery cinnamon-sugar filling are wonderfully fluffy—just like the classic Swedish Kanelbullar.
(See picture on page 136.)

TOTAL TIME	PREPARATION TIME	FERMENTATION TIME	TIME ON BAKING DAY
16.5–22 hours	50 minutes	2–4 hours (sourdough) + 13.5–17 hours (total dough)	3–4.5 hours

FOR THE LIEVITO MADRE

30 g Lievito Madre starter
15 g warm water (104 °F [40 °C])
30 g Type-550 wheat flour

FOR THE MAIN DOUGH

250–280 g cold whole milk
Mature Lievito Madre
5 g fresh yeast
1 cold medium egg
60 g sugar
10 g bourbon vanilla sugar
1 pinch ground cardamom (optional)
450 g Type-550 wheat flour
5 g salt
70 g cool butter

1. Whisk the Lievito Madre starter with the warm water until frothy. Then knead with the flour. Cover the Lievito Madre and allow it to ferment at 78–86 °F (26–30 °C) for **2–4 hours** until it has doubled in size.

2. Mix all ingredients for the main dough, except salt and butter, in a stand mixer or kneading machine on low speed for **10 minutes**. Start with the lower amount of whole milk. Then knead at a higher speed for **5–8 minutes**, gradually adding the salt and butter in portions, as well as up to 30 g more whole milk if needed.
   Dough weight: approx. 1,000 g
   Dough temperature after kneading: 75–79 °F (24–26 °C)

THE DAY BEFORE
6:00 PM
Prepare Lievito Madre

8:30 PM
Prepare the main dough

10:00 PM
Put in the refrigerator

ON BAKING DAY
10.00 AM
Take out of the refrigerator

11.30 AM
Shape and fill

1:00 PM
Preheat oven

134 ARTISAN SOURDOUGH: BREAD AND BEYOND

ADDITIONAL ITEMS

Neutral vegetable oil for the bowl/container

Flour for working

FOR THE FILLING

90 g very soft butter

60 g brown cane sugar

1 Tbsp. cinnamon powder (Ceylon cinnamon)

1 pinch ground cardamom

FOR THE EGG WASH AND TOPPING

1 egg

1 pinch sugar

1 pinch salt

Sugar crystals for sprinkling

Bulk fermentation

3. Let the dough rest, covered, in a lightly oiled bowl or proofing container at room temperature for about **1 hour**. Then place in the refrigerator at 41–43 °F (5–6 °C) for **10–12 hours**. Afterward, let the dough acclimate at room temperature for **1–2 hours**.

Shaping and filling

4. Place the acclimatized dough on a lightly floured work surface and carefully roll it out into a rectangle measuring approximately 12 x 16 inches to 16 x 20 inches (30 x 40 cm to 40 x 50 cm). Try not to apply too much pressure.

5. Evenly spread the soft butter over the rolled-out dough, leaving a ½ inch (2 cm) border all around. Mix the brown sugar with the cinnamon and cardamom, then sprinkle it over the butter.

6. Roll up the dough from the long side and cut into 12 equal pieces. Place them on two baking sheets lined with parchment paper or a reusable baking mat.

Final proof

7. Cover and let proof at room temperature for about **1.5–2 hours**.

8. For the egg wash, whisk the egg with salt and sugar, strain through a sieve, and brush the buns with it. Finally, sprinkle with sugar crystals.

Baking

9. Preheat the oven to 250 °F (180 °C) top/bottom heat. Bake the cinnamon buns one tray at a time on the lower third rack of the oven at 250 °F (180 °C) top/bottom heat for about **15–20 minutes** until golden brown. (At 320 °F [160 °C] convection, both trays can be baked simultaneously.) Allow to cool to at least lukewarm before serving.

1:30 PM
Apply icing + bake

1:50 PM
Remove from the oven

Swedish Cinnamon Rolls (page 134).

Plum Cake with Crumble (page 138).

Makes 1 Baking Sheet | Wheat Starter

PLUM CAKE WITH CRUMBLE

This juicy, tray-baked cake with cinnamon crumbles can also be varied: simply use other fruits instead of plums. (See picture on page 137.)

TOTAL TIME	PREPARATION TIME	FERMENTATION TIME	BAKING TIME
6–7.5 hours	50 minutes	5–6 hours (total dough)	30–40 minutes

FOR THE MAIN DOUGH

200 g cold whole milk
60 g cold liquid cream
100 g cold wheat sourdough starter
8 g fresh yeast
60 g sugar
10 g bourbon vanilla sugar
1 medium egg
450 g Type-550 wheat flour
5 g salt
60 g cool butter

FOR THE CRUMBLE DOUGH

250 g Type-405 wheat flour
150 g cold butter
90 g sugar
10 g bourbon vanilla sugar
½ tsp. cinnamon powder
1 pinch grated tonka bean (optional)
1 pinch salt

1. Mix all ingredients for the main dough, except salt and butter, in a stand mixer or kneading machine on low speed for **10 minutes**.

2. Knead at a higher speed for **5–8 minutes**, gradually adding the salt and butter in portions.
   Dough weight: approx. 1,000 g
   Dough temperature after kneading: 75–79 °F (24–26 °C)

3. For the crumble dough, briefly knead all ingredients together until a crumbly dough forms. Cover the crumble dough and place it in the refrigerator until further processing.

ON BAKING DAY

8:00 AM	8:30 AM	12:00 PM	1:30 PM	2:00 PM	2:35 PM
Prepare the main dough	Prepare crumble dough	Shaping + final proof	Preheat oven	Top and bake	Remove from the oven

ARTISAN SOURDOUGH: BREAD AND BEYOND

ADDITIONAL ITEMS

Neutral vegetable oil for the bowl/container
Flour for working
Fat for the tray (optional)

FOR THE TOPPING

4 lbs plums plums
30–50 g sugar (depending on the sweetness of the plums)
½ tsp. cinnamon powder

Bulk fermentation

4. Let the main dough rise, covered, in a lightly oiled bowl or proofing container at room temperature for **3–4 hours** until nearly doubled in size.

Shaping

5. Optionally, place the dough on a greased or parchment-lined deep baking sheet. Gently stretch it into a rectangle with your hands. (Alternatively, the dough can be rolled out carefully.)

Final proof

6. Cover and let the dough rise at room temperature for about **2 hours**.

7. For the topping, wash the plums, remove the stones and halve or quarter them. Then spread them evenly over the dough. Mix the sugar and cinnamon and sprinkle on top.
Finally, crumble the crumble dough evenly over the plums.

Baking

8. Preheat the oven to 320 °F (160 °C) with convection.
Bake the treats on the lower third rack of the oven at 320 °F (160 °C) convection for **30–40 minutes**.
Allow to cool to at least lukewarm before serving.

> **TIP**
> With a refreshed or very active wheat sourdough, the yeast amount can be reduced to 6 g.

Makes 10 Cookies | Lievito Madre

BLUEBERRY QUARK COOKIES

These pastries are wonderfully moist: a fine-textured, yeast-free dough with a fruity filling of quark and blueberries.

TOTAL TIME
7.5–9.5 hours

PREPARATION TIME
1 hour

FERMENTATION TIME
2–4 hours (sourdough) + 4.5 hours (total dough)

TIME ON BAKING DAY
7.5–9.5 hours

FOR THE LIEVITO MADRE
60 g Lievito Madre starter
(it should be very active and the last refreshment should be no more than 12 hours ago; better to refresh it again beforehand)
40 g warm whole milk (104°F [40°C])
60 g Type-550 wheat flour

FOR THE MAIN DOUGH
250 g cold whole milk
Mature Lievito Madre
60 g sugar
10 g bourbon vanilla sugar
1 cold medium egg
400 g Type-550 wheat flour
5 g salt
80 g cool butter

1. Whisk the Lievito Madre starter with the whole milk until frothy. Then knead with the flour. Cover the Lievito Madre and allow it to ferment at 78–86 °F (26–30 °C) for **2–4 hours** until it has doubled in size.

2. Mix all ingredients for the main dough, except salt and butter, in a stand mixer or kneading machine on low speed for **10 minutes**. Then knead at a higher speed for **5–8 minutes**, gradually adding the salt and butter in portions.
   Dough weight: approx. 1,010 g
   Dough temperature after kneading: 75–79 °F (24–26 °C)

ON BAKING DAY

8:00 AM Prepare Lievito Madre

10.00 AM Prepare the main dough

12.30 PM Shaping + final proof

2:30 PM Preheat oven

3:00 PM Fill and bake

3:15 PM Remove from the oven

ADDITIONAL ITEMS
Neutral vegetable oil for the bowl/container
Liquid cream for spreading

FOR THE FILLING
200 g fresh blueberries
200 g quark (20% fat)
30 g sugar
10 g bourbon vanilla sugar
½ tsp. zest of an untreated lemon
2 egg yolks
10 g cornstarch

Bulk fermentation

3. Let the dough rise, covered, in a lightly oiled bowl or proofing container at 77–81 °F (25–27 °C) for about **2 hours** until nearly doubled in size.

Shaping

4. Divide the dough into ten portions of about 100 g each. Carefully shape into rounds and let rest for **20–30 minutes**.

5. Then gently stretch the dough pieces to form small flatbreads. Place them on two baking sheets lined with parchment paper or a reusable baking mat.

Final proof

6. Cover and let proof at room temperature for about **2 hours**, gently stretching them again to a diameter of 6–7 inches (15–18 cm) after **1 hour**.

7. For the filling, wash the blueberries, sort them, and pat them dry. Mix the remaining ingredients thoroughly. First spread the quark cream mixture and then the blueberries in the middle of the dough, leaving a border of at least ½ inch (2 cm) free. Brush the outer edge of the dough with some cream.

Baking

8. Preheat the oven to 250 °F (180 °C) top/bottom heat well in advance.
Bake the pastries one at a time, steaming immediately, on the lower third rack of the oven at 250 °F (180 °C) top/bottom heat for **15–20 minutes**. Do not release the steam throughout the baking process. (At 320 °F (160 °C) convection, both sheets can be baked simultaneously.) Allow to cool to at least lukewarm before serving.

BLUEBERRY QUARK COOKIES | 143

Makes 1 Cake (loaf pan, about 12 x 4 inches [30 x 11 cm]) | Wheat starter

SOURDOUGH BABKA

This aromatic sourdough cake with a long fermentation time comes in two variations: either with a fruity sour cherry filling or a nut-nougat cream.

TOTAL TIME	PREPARATION TIME	FERMENTATION TIME	BAKING TIME
26–34 hours	1 hour	6–9 hours (sourdough, total) + 18–24 hours (total dough)	30–40 minutes

FOR THE FLOUR DOUGH
80 g milk
15 g Type-550 wheat flour

FOR THE SOURDOUGH STAGE 1
10 g wheat starter (it should be very active and the last refreshment should not have been more than 12 hours ago)
20 g warm water (104°F [40°C])
20 g Type-550 wheat flour

FOR THE SOURDOUGH STAGE 2
Entire sourdough from stage 1
50 g warm coffee (104°F [40°C])
50 g Type-550 wheat flour

1. Whisk the milk and wheat flour in a saucepan until smooth and lump-free. Heat slowly and continue stirring. After a few minutes the mixture begins to thicken like pudding. Transfer to another container and let cool for a few minutes. Then cover the flour dough with plastic wrap and refrigerate for at least **2 hours**.

2. For the sourdough stage 1, thoroughly mix the wheat starter with the warm water and flour. Cover the sourdough and let rise at 78–86 °F (26–30 °C) for **4–6 hours** until well doubled.

3. For the sourdough stage 2, mix the entire sourdough from stage 1 thoroughly with the warm coffee and wheat flour. Cover the sourdough and let rise at 79–86 °F (26–30 °C) for **2–3 hours** until well doubled.

THE DAY BEFORE

9:00 AM	9:30 AM	1:00 PM	3:00 PM	4:30 PM	5:30 PM
Prepare sourdough stage 1	*Prepare flour dough*	*Prepare sourdough stage 2*	*Prepare the main dough*	*Stretch and fold*	*Stretch and fold*

144 ARTISAN SOURDOUGH: BREAD AND BEYOND

FOR THE MAIN DOUGH

Cold flour dough

Mature sourdough

150 g sweet cream

1 cold medium egg

50 g sugar

10 g bourbon vanilla sugar

385 g Type-550 wheat flour

30 g baking cocoa

5 g salt

20 g whole milk (as needed)

ADDITIONAL ITEMS

Neutral vegetable oil for the bowl/container

Fat for the mold

Flour for working

FOR THE FILLING AND TOPPING

350 g sour cherry fruit spread (70% fruit content) or alternatively 250–300 g nut-nougat cream

Liquid cream for spreading

Powdered sugar for dusting

4. Mix all ingredients for the main dough, except salt and whole milk, in a stand mixer or kneading machine on low speed for 10 minutes. Then knead at a higher setting for 5–8 minutes. Knead in the salt and, if necessary, up to 20 g of whole milk.

   Dough weight: approx. 940 g

   Dough temperature after kneading: 75–79 °F (24–26 °C)

Bulk fermentation

5. Let the dough rest covered in a lightly oiled bowl or container at 79–82 °F (26–28 °C) for about **4–5 hours** until doubled in size, stretching and folding after **1 hour** and **2 hours**.

Shaping and filling

6. Grease a loaf pan well. Place the risen dough on a lightly floured work surface and gently stretch it into a rectangle of about 16 x 16 inches (40 x 40 cm) or roll it out with minimal pressure.

7. Spread the sour cherry fruit spread or, alternatively, the nut-nougat cream evenly over the rolled-out dough, leaving a ½ inch (2 cm) border around the edges.

8. Slice the filled dough roll lengthwise down the middle, leaving the top end uncut to keep the strands connected when twisting. Twist the resulting dough strands together like a cord and place them in the prepared loaf pan.

Final proof

9. Let the shaped dough proof at 79–82 °F (26–28 °C) for about **60–80 minutes** [alternatively, at 72–75 °F (22–24 °C) for about **2 hours**]. Then refrigerate at 43–46 °F (6–8 °C) for **12–16 hours**. Afterward, allow it to acclimate at room temperature for **60–80 minutes**.

ON BAKING DAY

8:00 PM
Shape and fill + ferment

9:45 PM
Put in the refrigerator

12:00 PM
Take out of the refrigerator

1:40 PM
Preheat oven

2:10 PM
Spread with cream and bake

ARTISAN SOURDOUGH: BREAD AND BEYOND

Baking

10. Preheat the oven to 392 °F (200 °C) top/bottom heat well in advance.

11. Brush the dough with a little cream. Then place it in the oven, steam immediately (see page 31), and reduce the temperature to 250 °F (180 °C).
Bake the Babka for about **30–40 minutes** in total, keeping the steam inside throughout the baking time. Cover if browning too quickly.

12. After baking, let the Babka rest in the loaf pan for about **5 minutes**, then carefully remove it and let it cool at least until lukewarm on a wire rack. Dust with powdered sugar before serving.

2:45 PM
Remove from the oven

2:50 PM
Remove from the mold

SOURDOUGH BABKA | 147

Makes 2 Pieces | Wheat Starter

YEAST BRAID WITH MILK SOURDOUGH

This classic sweet, braided yeast bread is prepared in a variation with minimal yeast, mild sourdough, and a long fermentation in the refrigerator. (See picture on page 150.)

TOTAL TIME	PREPARATION TIME	FERMENTATION TIME	TIME ON BAKING DAY
18–23 hours	1 hour	2–4 hours (sourdough) + 15–18 (total dough)	30 minutes

FOR THE MILK SOURDOUGH
50 g wheat starter
50 g warm whole milk (104°F [40°C])
50 g Type-550 wheat flour

FOR THE FLOUR DOUGH
100 g whole milk
20 g Type-550 wheat flour

FOR THE MAIN DOUGH
Flour dough
Mature milk sourdough
100 g cold whole milk
5 g fresh yeast
1 medium egg
1 egg yolk
70 g sugar
10 g bourbon vanilla sugar
1 tsp. zest from an untreated lemon
400 g Type-550 wheat flour
5 g salt
70 g cold butter

1. For the milk sourdough, dissolve the wheat starter in the warm milk and then mix thoroughly with the wheat flour. Cover the milk sourdough and allow it to ferment at 78–86 °F (26–30 °C) for **2–4 hours** until it has doubled in size.

2. For the flour dough, whisk the whole milk and flour in a saucepan until smooth and lump-free. Heat slowly and continue stirring. After a few minutes the mixture begins to thicken like pudding. Transfer to another container and let cool for a few minutes. Then cover the flour dough with plastic wrap and refrigerate for at least **2 hours**.

3. Mix all ingredients for the main dough, except salt and butter, in a stand mixer or kneading machine on low speed for **10 minutes**. Then knead at a higher speed for **5–8 minutes**, gradually incorporating the salt and butter in portions.
   Dough weight: approx. 990 g
   Dough temperature after kneading: 75–79 °F (24–26 °C)

THE DAY BEFORE

1:30 PM	1:40 PM	4:00 PM	5:30 PM	7:30 PM	7:45 PM
Prepare milk sourdough	Prepare flour dough	Prepare the main dough	Stretch and fold	Weigh and form round	Pre-shape

148 ARTISAN SOURDOUGH: BREAD AND BEYOND

ADDITIONAL ITEMS

Neutral vegetable oil for the bowl/container

Bulk fermentation

4. Let the dough rise in a lightly oiled bowl or container at room temperature for about **3–4 hours**, covered, until doubled in size, stretching and folding after **1 hour**.

Shaping

5. Divide the dough into six pieces of about 165–170 g each. Shape them into tight rounds and let them rest, covered, for **15 minutes** with the seam side down. Then flip them over, fold each into a cylinder, and roll into a strand about 6 inches (15 cm) long. Cover and let rest for another **15 minutes**. Afterward, roll the dough pieces into strands about 12 inches (30 cm) long. Braid three strands of dough.

Final proof

6. Cover and let them proof at room temperature for **1.5 hours**. Then refrigerate at 41–43 °F (5–6 °C) for **10–12 hours**. Afterward, let them acclimate for about **20 minutes**.

FOR THE EGG WASH AND TOPPING

1 egg white
1 pinch salt
1 pinch sugar
Sugar crystals for sprinkling
Sliced almonds for sprinkling

7. For the egg wash, whisk the egg white with salt and sugar, strain through a sieve, and brush onto the braids. Finally, sprinkle with sugar crystals and sliced almonds.

Baking

8. Preheat the oven to 392 °F (200 °C) top/bottom heat well in advance.

9. Put the braids in the oven, immediately add a little steam and reduce the temperature to 338 °F (170 °C) top/bottom heat. Bake for a total of **25–30 minutes** until golden brown. Do not let the steam out during the entire baking time and cover the braids in time if they brown too much.
Allow to cool to at least lukewarm before serving.

8:00 PM
Braid

9:30 PM
Put in the refrigerator

ON BAKING DAY
8:00 AM
Preheat the oven and take the yeast plaits out of the fridge

8.20 AM
Apply icing + bake

8.45 AM
Remove from the oven

Yeast Braid with Milk Sourdough (page 148).

Buchteln (Sweet Rolls) (page 152).

Makes 12 Rolls (baking dish about 12 x 8 inches [30 x 20 cm]) | Lievito Madre

BUCHTELN (SWEET ROLLS)

These sweet yeast dumplings, filled with apricot jam, are often served with vanilla sauce or fruit compote. (See picture on page 151.)

TOTAL TIME	PREPARATION TIME	FERMENTATION TIME	TIME ON BAKING DAY
18–23 hours	1 hour	2–4 hours (sourdough) + 15–18 hours (total dough)	60–70 minutes

FOR THE LIEVITO MADRE
20 g warm whole milk (104°F [40°C])
30 g Lievito Madre starter
30 g Type-550 wheat flour

1. Whisk the Lievito Madre starter with the milk until foamy. Then knead with the flour. Cover the Lievito Madre and allow it to ferment at 78–86°F (26–30°C) for **2–4 hours** until it has doubled in size.

FOR THE MAIN DOUGH
260 g cold whole milk
Mature Lievito Madre
5 g fresh yeast
40 g sugar
10 g bourbon vanilla sugar
1 tsp. zest from an untreated lemon
4 egg yolks
450 g Type-550 wheat flour
5 g salt
75 g cool butter

2. Mix all ingredients for the main dough, except salt and butter, in a stand mixer or kneading machine on low speed for **10 minutes**. Then knead at a higher setting for **5–8 minutes**. Knead in salt and butter in portions.
   Dough weight: approx. 980 g
   Dough temperature after kneading: 75–79°F (24–26°C)

THE DAY BEFORE
2:00 PM Prepare Lievito Madre
4:30 PM Prepare the main dough
8:30 PM Shape
8:50 PM Fill + brush with cream
10:00 PM Put in the refrigerator

ARTISAN SOURDOUGH: BREAD AND BEYOND

ADDITIONAL ITEMS

Neutral vegetable oil for the bowl/container

Butter for the mold

FOR THE FILLING AND TOPPING

250 g apricot jam

Liquid cream for brushing

Powdered sugar for dusting (optional)

> **TIP**
>
> The recipe can also be used to prepare yeast dumplings. For this variation, the dough is filled with plum mousse instead of apricot jam, and the shaped dumplings are steamed instead of baked after the final proof. Then serve the yeast dumplings with ground poppy seeds, powdered sugar, and melted butter or vanilla sauce.

Bulk fermentation

3. Let the dough rise in a lightly oiled bowl or container at room temperature, covered, for about **3–4 hours** until doubled in size.

Shaping and filling

4. Divide the proofed dough into twelve portions of about 80 g each and gently shape them into rounds. Cover and let rest with the dough seam facing down for **15–20 minutes**. (Process the dough with little-to-no flour to ensure the seams hold together well later.)

5. Then turn the dough pieces over, gently press them flat and place a walnut-sized amount of apricot jam in the middle of each one. Seal the dough tightly around the filling, pressing the seam firmly.

6. Place the dough pieces seam side down, in a buttered baking dish and brush them with a little cream.

Final proof

7. Let them proof while covered at room temperature for **1 hour**. Then refrigerate at 41–43 °F (5–6 °C) for **10–12 hours**. Then brush some more cream on top and let it acclimatize for **30 minutes**.

Baking

8. Preheat the oven to 392 °F (200 °C) top/bottom heat well in advance.
   Put the sweet treats in the oven, immediately add a little steam and reduce the temperature to 338 °F (170 °C) top/bottom heat. Bake for a total of **30–40 minutes** until golden brown, making sure the steam is not released during the entire baking time. Then allow to cool to at least lukewarm. Dust with powdered sugar before serving if desired.

ON BAKING DAY

8:30 AM
Take out of the refrigerator + preheat oven

9:00 AM
Bake

9.35 AM
Remove from the oven

BUCHTELN (SWEET ROLLS)

Makes 1 Pie (springform pan, 10 inches [26 cm] diameter) | Wheat Starter

FERMENTED APPLE PIE

What makes this simple and moist apple pie with almonds special is all the flour that is first fermented in a milk sourdough.

TOTAL TIME
4–6 hours

PREPARATION TIME
30 minutes

FERMENTATION TIME
3–5 hours (sourdough)

BAKING TIME
40 minutes

FOR THE MILK SOURDOUGH
80 g wheat starter
200 g lukewarm whole milk (104°F [40°C])
200 g Type-405 wheat flour

FOR THE TOPPING
4 apples of your choice
1 tsp. lemon juice

FOR THE MAIN DOUGH
90 g soft butter
1 pinch salt
120 g sugar
10 g bourbon vanilla sugar
2 tsp. zest from an untreated lemon
3 medium eggs
Mature milk sourdough
1 tsp. baking powder

ADDITIONAL ITEMS
2 Tbsp. cinnamon sugar
40 g sliced almonds
Powdered sugar for dusting

1. Dissolve the sourdough starter in the full milk and then mix thoroughly with the wheat flour. Cover the milk sourdough and allow it to ferment at 78–86°F (26–30°C) for **3–5 hours** until it has doubled in size.

2. Preheat the oven to 250°F (180°C) top/bottom heat. Line a springform pan with baking paper.

3. For the topping, peel, core, and dice the apples (about ½ inch [2 cm] in size). Mix with the lemon juice and set aside.

4. For the main dough, beat the butter with the salt, sugar, and bourbon vanilla sugar until light and creamy. Add the lemon zest and the eggs one at a time, mixing well. Then briefly fold in the mature milk sourdough and baking powder.

5. Spread the dough evenly in the prepared springform pan. Place the diced apples on the dough. Finally, sprinkle with cinnamon sugar and then with the sliced almonds.

Baking

6. Bake the apple pie in the lower third of the preheated oven at 250°F (180°C) top/bottom heat for about **50 minutes**. Let it cool in the baking pan and dust with powdered sugar before serving.

Makes 1 Loaf (springform pan, 11–12 inches [28–30 cm] diameter) | Lievito Madre

BANANA BREAD

The American banana bread is a moist cake and a great way to use up overripe bananas.

TOTAL TIME
70–80 minutes

PREPARATION TIME
20 minutes

BAKING TIME
50–60 minutes

FOR THE DOUGH

4 very ripe bananas (approx. 350 g, peeled)
1 Tbsp. lemon juice
150 g Lievito Madre starter
4 medium eggs
80 g sugar
80 g brown cane sugar
1 pinch salt
125 g canola oil
200 g Type-405 wheat flour
1.5 tsp. baking powder
¼ tsp. baking soda
½ tsp. cinnamon powder
100 g walnut kernels

ADDITIONAL ITEMS

Fat for the mold
Flour for the mold (optional)
1 banana (optional)

1. Preheat the oven to 250 °F (180 °C) top/bottom heat. Grease a loaf pan and either lightly flour it or line it with baking paper.

2. For the dough, puree the bananas with the lemon juice and the Lievito Madre starter in a blender or with an immersion blender. Whisk the eggs with the sugar, cane sugar, and salt until frothy. Stir in the banana puree and canola oil. Mix the flour with baking powder, baking soda, and cinnamon, then briefly fold it in. Finally, roughly chop the walnuts and fold them in.

3. Pour the dough into the prepared loaf pan. Optionally, peel a banana, slice it lengthwise, and place it on top of the dough.

Baking

4. Bake the banana bread in the lower third of the preheated oven at 250 °F (180 °C) top/bottom heat for about **50–60 minutes**. Then let it rest in the mold for about **10 minutes**. Next, remove the banana bread from the pan, let it cool completely on a wire rack, and serve.

> **TIP**
> Additionally, 1g of baking-stable dark chocolate chunks can be folded into the dough together with the walnuts.

ARTISAN SOURDOUGH: BREAD AND BEYOND

Makes 12 Muffins | Wheat Starter

RASPBERRY WHITE CHOCOLATE MUFFINS

These muffins are super quick and very easy to prepare.

TOTAL TIME
40 minutes

PREPARATION TIME
15 minutes

BAKING TIME
25 minutes

FOR THE DOUGH

160 g whole milk yogurt
120 g wheat starter
90 g canola oil
2 medium eggs
1 tsp. zest from an untreated lemon
200 g Type-405 wheat flour
150 g sugar
1 tsp. baking powder
½ tsp. baking soda
1 pinch salt
100 g white chocolate
200 g frozen raspberries

ADDITIONAL ITEMS

Powdered sugar for dusting (optional)

1. Preheat the oven to 250 °F (180 °C) top/bottom heat. Line a twelve-cup muffin tin with paper liners.

2. For the dough, mix the whole milk yogurt, rye starter, canola oil, eggs, and lemon zest in a large bowl until smooth.

3. In a separate bowl, combine the wheat flour, sugar, baking powder, baking soda, and salt. Briefly fold the dry mixture into the yogurt-sourdough mixture.

4. Roughly chop the white chocolate and quickly fold it into the mix along with the raspberries. Distribute the mixture evenly into the muffin liners, using an ice cream scoop for easy portioning.

Baking

5. Bake the muffins in the lower third of the preheated oven at 250 °F (180 °C) top/bottom heat for about **25 minutes**. Let the muffins rest in the tin for about **10 minutes**, then remove them from the tin and allow them to cool completely on a wire rack. Let them cool completely. Before serving, dust with powdered sugar as desired.

TIP

Instead of 120 g wheat starter, Lievito Madre starter can also be used. For this, mix 90 g Lievito Madre starter with 30 g milk or water before making the dough.

158 ARTISAN SOURDOUGH: BREAD AND BEYOND

Makes 12 Brownies (baking pan, about 9 x 9 inches [23 x 23 cm]) | Rye Starter

FUDGY BROWNIES

Brownies—a simple and moist chocolate cake.

TOTAL TIME
40–45 minutes

PREPARATION TIME
20 minutes

BAKING TIME
20–25 minutes

FOR THE DOUGH
250 g dark chocolate
200 g soft butter
150 g brown cane sugar
50 g beet syrup
1 pinch salt
4 medium eggs
100 g rye starter
150 g Type-405 wheat flour
40 g baking cocoa

1. Preheat the oven to 250 °F (180 °C) top/bottom heat. Line a square baking pan with baking paper.

2. Finely chop the dark chocolate. Combine with butter, brown cane sugar, molasses, and salt in a saucepan and melt over low heat. Then pour into a large bowl.

3. Whisk in the eggs one at a time, then stir in the rye starter. Finally, fold in the flour and cocoa.

   Baking
4. Bake the brownies in the lower third of the oven at 250 °F (180 °C) top/bottom heat for about **20–25 minutes**. Let them cool completely. Then remove from the tin using the baking paper, cut into 12 squares, and serve.

Makes 1 Cake (springform pan, 10 inches [26 cm] diameter) | Rye Starter

TORTA DI NOCCIOLE

Torta di Nocciole is a moist Piedmontese hazelnut cake with chocolate.

TOTAL TIME
1.5 hours

PREPARATION TIME
30 minutes

BAKING TIME
50 minutes

FOR THE DOUGH
250 g roasted hazelnuts
150 g dark chocolate
6 medium or large eggs
150 g soft butter
140 g sugar
10 g bourbon vanilla sugar
100 g rye starter
1 pinch salt

ADDITIONAL ITEMS
Powdered sugar for dusting

1. Preheat the oven to 338 °F (170 °C) top/bottom heat. Line a springform pan with baking paper.

2. For the dough, finely chop the hazelnuts. Break the chocolate into pieces and melt it over a water bath in a double broiler, then set aside to cool slightly.

3. Then separate the eggs. Using a hand mixer, beat the butter with 70 g sugar and the bourbon vanilla sugar until light and creamy. Stir in the egg yolks one at a time. Fold in the finely chopped hazelnuts, melted chocolate, and rye starter.

4. In a clean, grease-free bowl, beat the egg whites with a pinch of salt using a hand or stand mixer, gradually adding the remaining sugar. Continue beating until the sugar is fully dissolved. Gently fold the beaten egg whites into the hazelnut-chocolate mixture.
Spread the dough evenly in the prepared springform pan.

Baking

5. Bake the cake in the lower third of the preheated oven at 338 °F (170 °C) top/bottom heat for about **50 minutes**, keeping the oven door closed during baking. After baking, slightly open the oven door and let the cake cool for **10 minutes**. Then remove it from the oven and allow it to cool completely in the pan. Before serving, sprinkle the Torta di Nocciole with some powdered sugar.

> **TIP**
> This cake tastes especially delicious when served with a scoop of vanilla ice cream.

ARTISAN SOURDOUGH: BREAD AND BEYOND

Makes 1 Cake (springform pan, 10 inches [26 cm] diameter) | Lievito Madre

TORTA DI MANDORLE

Torta di Mandorle is a moist Sicilian almond cake, enhanced with citrus aromas and Amaretto.

TOTAL TIME
1.5 hours

PREPARATION TIME
30 minutes

BAKING TIME
50 minutes

FOR THE DOUGH

6 medium or large eggs
150 g soft butter
150 g sugar
250 g ground almonds
2 tsp. zest of an untreated orange
1 tsp. zest from an untreated lemon
75 g Lievito Madre starter
25 g Amaretto
1 pinch salt

ADDITIONAL ITEMS

40 g sliced almonds
Powdered sugar for dusting

1. Preheat the oven to 250 °F (180 °C) top/bottom heat. Line a springform pan with baking paper.

2. For the dough, separate the eggs. Using a hand mixer, beat the butter and 75 g sugar until light and creamy. Stir in the egg yolks one at a time. Mix in the ground almonds, orange zest, and lemon zest. Stir the Lievito Madre starter and Amaretto until smooth and mix thoroughly into the egg yolk mixture.

3. In a clean, grease-free bowl, beat the egg whites with a pinch of salt using a hand or stand mixer, gradually adding the remaining sugar. Continue beating until the sugar is fully dissolved. Gently fold the beaten egg whites into the butter-almond mixture.
Spread the dough evenly in the prepared springform pan and sprinkle with the sliced almonds.

Baking

4. Bake the cake in the lower third of the preheated oven at 250 °F (180 °C) top/bottom heat for about **50 minutes**, keeping the oven door closed during baking. Then slightly open the oven door and let the cake cool for **10 minutes**. Remove the Torta di Mandorle from the oven and allow it to cool completely in the pan. Before serving, dust with powdered sugar.

TIP

For a special touch, mix 1 Tbsp. Amaretto with 3 Tbsp. orange marmalade and heat in a small saucepan. After baking, brush the warm cake with this glaze using a pastry brush.

Makes 18 Brookies | Rye Starter

BROOKIES

A delicious combination of brownies and cookies: soft and extra chocolaty cookies with a soft center.

TOTAL TIME	PREPARATION TIME	RESTING TIME	BAKING TIME
1 hour	15 minutes	30 minutes	10–14 minutes

FOR THE DOUGH
200 g dark chocolate (70% cocoa content)
50 g butter
50 g brown cane sugar
1 medium egg
75 g sugar
1 pinch salt
120 g rye starter
10 g baking cocoa
½ tsp. baking powder

1. Finely chop the dark chocolate. Place it in a saucepan with the butter and brown sugar and melt over low heat. Let the mixture cool for a few minutes.

2. Beat the egg with the sugar and salt until creamy. Then fold in the sourdough starter and the chocolate mixture. Finally, mix the cocoa powder with the baking powder and fold it in. Place the dough in the refrigerator for about **30 minutes**.

3. Using two teaspoons, scoop cookie-sized portions of dough and place them on two parchment-lined baking sheets, leaving enough space between them.

Baking

4. Preheat the oven to 320°F (160°C) convection heat.
Bake the cookies in the preheated oven for about **10–14 minutes**. Let them cool on the baking sheet before serving.

TIP
Instead of the rye starter, you can also mix 90 g Lievito Madre starter with 30 g espresso or whole milk until smooth and fold it into the dough.

Makes 1 Cake (springform pan, 10 inches [26 cm] diameter) | Rye Starter and Wheat Starter

CHOCOLATE-CHERRY CHEESECAKE WITH CRUMBLE

This cheesecake is a true classic, prepared here with two types of sourdough and a creamy quark filling with cherries.

TOTAL TIME	PREPARATION TIME	BAKING TIME
1.5 hours	30 minutes	1 hour

FOR THE DOUGH
- 300 g Type-405 wheat flour
- 200 g cold butter, in pieces
- 150 g sugar
- 100 g rye starter
- 40 g baking cocoa
- 1 tsp. baking powder
- 1 egg yolk

ADDITIONAL ITEMS
- Fat for the mold

FOR THE FILLING
- 1 medium egg
- 1 egg white
- 90 g sugar
- 10 g bourbon vanilla sugar
- 1 pinch salt
- ½ untreated lemon
- 250 g low-fat quark
- 250 g sour cream
- 100 g wheat starter
- 1 jar sour cherries (680 g), drained

1. Preheat the oven to 250 °F (180 °C) top/bottom heat. Line the bottom of a springform pan with parchment paper and lightly grease the sides.

2. Quickly knead the dough ingredients into a shortcrust pastry. Chill about one-third of the dough in the refrigerator for at least **30 minutes**.

3. Press the remaining dough into the springform pan, forming a rim about 1 ½ inch (4 cm) high. The dough can be carefully rolled out on a lightly floured work surface or spread out in the pan with your hands and pressed down firmly. Prick the base several times with a fork and chill the dough until further processing.

4. For the filling, mix the egg and egg white with the sugar, bourbon vanilla sugar, and salt. Wash and dry the lemon. Grate the zest, squeeze the juice, and add both to the egg mixture. Finally, stir in the quark, sour cream, and wheat starter until smooth.

5. Pour about two-thirds of the quark mixture onto the dough base. Spread the drained cherries on top and pour the remaining quark mixture over it. Sprinkle the remaining dough from the fridge over the top as a crumble.

Baking

6. Bake the cheesecake in the lower third of the preheated oven at 250 °F (180 °C) top/bottom heat for about **1 hour**. Let it cool completely before serving or store it in the refrigerator.

SWEETS FOR BREAKFAST & DESSERT

Makes 1 Sheet | Rye Starter

GRANOLA

Homemade crunchy muesli: a crisp granola based on fermented oats.

TOTAL TIME
21–25 hours

PREPARATION TIME
20 minutes

FERMENTATION TIME
20–24 hours

BAKING TIME
40–50 minutes

FOR THE FERMENTED OATMEAL
100 g lukewarm coffee (86 °F [30 °C])
or oat/almond drink
50 g rye starter
250 g of whole grain oat flakes

FOR THE GRANOLA
100 g sliced hazelnuts
30 g shredded coconut
2 Tbsp. cocoa powder
Fermented oat flakes
60 g coconut oil
100 g maple syrup
10 g bourbon vanilla sugar
1 pinch salt
100 g dark chocolate or chocolate chips
100 g banana chips

> **TIP**
> The granola can also be varied with slivered almonds, white chocolate, and freeze-dried strawberries or raspberries.

1. Mix the coffee and the rye starter. Then mix with the oat flakes; the mixture should then be relatively dry.

2. Cover and let ferment at room temperature for **20–24 hours**, stirring briefly once after **10–12 hours**. The oats should be moist and aromatic at the end of the fermentation time.

3. Preheat the oven to 302 °F (150 °C) hot air/convection. Mix the hazelnuts, shredded coconut, and cocoa powder into the fermented oats.

4. For the granola, heat the coconut oil, maple syrup, bourbon vanilla sugar, and salt in a saucepan over medium heat until the coconut oil has melted. Then mix into the oatmeal mixture. Spread the granola on a baking tray lined with baking paper.

Baking

5. Roast in the lower third of a preheated oven at 302 °F (150 °C) convection for about **40–50 minutes**, keeping an eye on it. Stir occasionally and pay particular attention to the edge area as this is where it burns the fastest. The granola is ready when it is completely dry. If necessary, extend the baking time or allow to cool in the slightly open and switched off oven. After roasting, allow to cool completely.

Then coarsely chop the dark chocolate and banana chips, mix them in, and serve or store in an airtight container.

Makes 2–3 Servings | Wheat Starter

OVERNIGHT BAKED OATMEAL

*A combination of overnight oats and baked oats, also known as oatmeal.
Here the oat flakes are soaked overnight at room temperature, fermented, and baked.*

TOTAL TIME	PREPARATION TIME	FERMENTATION TIME	BAKING TIME
8.5–12.5 hours	10 minutes	8–12 hours	20–25 minutes

FOR THE OATMEAL

Coconut oil for the form
1 large banana
1 splash lemon juice
2–3 Tbsp. maple syrup or liquid honey
5 g wheat starter
240 g oat or almond milk
1 tsp. cinnamon powder
100 g rolled oats
30 g chopped walnuts

ADDITIONAL ITEMS

50 g frozen blueberries
4 Tbsp. whole milk yogurt
2 Tbsp. maple syrup or liquid honey

1. Grease a baking dish 8 x 6 inches (20 × 15 cm) or two to three small oven dishes with a little coconut oil.

2. Peel the banana, mash or puree it with the lemon juice. Then mix thoroughly with the maple syrup and wheat starter. Add the oat milk and cinnamon as well as the oat flakes and walnuts and mix well. Pour the mixture into the dish(es) and let sit covered at room temperature for about **8–12 hours** overnight.

3. The next morning, preheat the oven to 250 °F (180 °C) top/bottom heat. Distribute the blueberries evenly over the oat mixture.

Baking

4. Bake in the lower third of the preheated oven at 250 °F (180 °C) top/bottom heat; baking time is about **20–25 minutes** in a baking dish, or about **15 minutes** in small ramekins.
Top the oatmeal with whole milk yogurt and maple syrup before serving.

Makes 20 Bars (baking dish about 8 x 12 inches [20 x 30 cm]) | Rye Starter

MUESLI BARS

These homemade muesli bars are the perfect snack for in between meals or on the go. And they're also quick and easy to make!

TOTAL TIME	PREPARATION TIME	BAKING TIME
40 minutes	15–20 minutes	20–25 minutes

FOR THE MUESLI BARS
- 100 g liquid honey
- 20 g brown cane sugar
- 60 g coconut oil
- 1 pinch salt
- 200 g muesli (e.g., chocolate muesli)
- 40 g puffed quinoa
- 40 g rolled oats
- 50 g chopped almonds, roasted
- 50 g chopped hazelnuts, roasted
- 30 g shredded coconut
- 100 g rye starter
- 100 g dried cherries
- 100 g baking-stable chocolate drops

1. Preheat the oven to 250 °F (180 °C) top/bottom heat. Line a baking dish with parchment paper, leaving an overhang on the sides.

2. Heat the honey, cane sugar, coconut oil, and salt in a saucepan over medium heat for **3–5 minutes** until the sugar dissolves.

3. In a large bowl, mix the muesli, quinoa, oats, almonds, hazelnuts, and shredded coconut. Pour the warm honey-coconut oil mixture over and mix quickly. Then add the rye starter and incorporate thoroughly. Finally, coarsely chop the cherries and fold them in along with the chocolate chips.

4. Transfer the mixture to the prepared baking dish. Place a piece of baking paper on top and press it down evenly with your hands. Then press down firmly again with the bottom of a glass. (The more compact the mixture, the better the granola bars will hold together.)

Baking

5. Bake in the lower third of a preheated oven at 250 °F (180 °C) top/bottom heat for about **20–25 minutes** until golden brown. Then allow to cool completely and lift it out of the tin using the excess baking paper.

6. Cut the mixture into bars using a sharp knife. Serve immediately or store in an airtight container.

Makes 4 Servings | Wheat Starter

PANCAKES

Pancakes are small, thick, and fluffy. They are often served for breakfast and pair well not only with sweet toppings like fresh fruit but also with maple syrup, crispy bacon, and fried or scrambled eggs.

TOTAL TIME
30 minutes

PREPARATION TIME
30 minutes

FOR THE DOUGH
200 g wheat starter
150 g whole milk
2 medium eggs
30 g butter, melted
100 g Type-405 wheat flour
1 ½ tsp. baking powder
¼ tsp. salt
1 Tbsp. sugar

ADDITIONAL ITEMS
Canola oil for frying
200 g bacon (sliced)
20 g butter
8 Tbsp. maple syrup

1. In a bowl, whisk together the wheat starter, milk, eggs, and melted butter until smooth.

2. Sift the flour and baking powder into a separate bowl. Add the salt and sugar and mix with the sourdough mixture to form a thick dough.

3. Heat a little canola oil in a pan. Use 2–3 Tbsp. of batter to bake small pancakes, each about 4 inches (10 cm) in diameter, turning the pancakes as soon as the batter starts to bubble on the top. Keep the finished pancakes warm until serving.

4. Fry the bacon in a pan without adding fat.
To serve, stack the pancakes and place a piece of butter on top. Finally, drizzle with maple syrup and serve the pancakes with the fried bacon.

> **TIP**
> Pancakes typically contain a relatively large amount of baking powder and baking soda. To reduce the baking powder amount to about ½ tsp., you can separate the eggs, whip the egg whites separately, and fold them into the batter at the end.

Makes 4 Servings | Wheat Starter

GRANDMA'S APPLE PANCAKES

These sweet pancakes with a fluffy batter and fresh apples are served with cinnamon sugar and are a true classic, loved by young and old alike.

TOTAL TIME	PREPARATION TIME	FERMENTATION TIME
3.5–5.5 hours	30 minutes	3–5 hours (sourdough)

FOR THE WHEAT-MILK SOURDOUGH
80 g wheat starter
160 g warm whole milk (104°F [40°C])
160 g Type-405 wheat flour

FOR THE MAIN DOUGH
2 eggs
Mature wheat-milk sourdough
50 g whole milk
10 g bourbon vanilla sugar
1 pinch salt
50 g sugar
2 large apples (e.g., Boskoop variety)

ADDITIONAL ITEMS
2–3 Tbsp. butter for frying
4 Tbsp. cinnamon sugar

1. Dissolve the sourdough starter in the whole milk and then mix thoroughly with the wheat flour. Let the mixture rise, covered, at 78–86 °F (26–30 °C) for **3–5 hours** until well doubled.

2. For the main batter, separate the eggs. Mix the egg yolks with the wheat-milk sourdough, whole milk, and bourbon vanilla sugar thoroughly.

3. Beat the egg whites and salt with a hand mixer or food processor in a clean, grease-free bowl until stiff. Add the sugar and continue beating until it has completely dissolved. Gently fold the beaten egg whites into the sourdough mixture.

4. Peel the apples, quarter them, and slice them finely or shave them with a grater. Briefly fold them into the pancake batter.

5. Heat some butter in a nonstick pan. Fry the batter in four batches on both sides until golden brown. Sprinkle the finished pancakes with cinnamon sugar and serve immediately.

TIP
Instead of the refreshed wheat-milk sourdough, a mild wheat starter can also be used. In that case, for a richer flavor, replace 50 g of milk with 50 g of liquid cream in the main batter.

Makes 2 Servings | Lievito Madre

DUTCH BABY

A Dutch Baby, also known as an oven-puffed pancake, is a pancake baked in a hot pan in the oven.

TOTAL TIME	PREPARATION TIME	BAKING TIME
30 minutes	30 minutes	15–18 minutes

FOR THE DOUGH
150 g Lievito Madre starter
125 g whole milk
3 medium eggs
30 g sugar
10 g bourbon vanilla sugar
1 pinch salt
20 g butter

ADDITIONAL ITEMS
40 g mixed berries (fresh or frozen)
Powdered sugar for dusting

TIP
Instead of 150 g of Lievito Madre starter, wheat starter can also be used.

In that case, use 200 g wheat starter and only 75 g milk (instead of 125 g) in the dough.

1. Place an oven-proof pan (9–10 inches [24–26 cm]) in diameter, preferably with slightly high sides and ideally made of cast iron) in the oven and preheat the oven to 428 °F (220 °C) top/bottom heat.

2. In the meantime, if using fresh berries, wash, sort, and pat them dry.

3. For the mix, whisk together the Lievito Madre starter and whole milk in a bowl until smooth. In a separate bowl, beat the eggs with the sugar, bourbon vanilla sugar, and salt until foamy. Combine the milk-Lievito Madre mixture with the beaten eggs.

4. Add the butter to the preheated pan and tilt it slightly to evenly distribute the melting butter. Immediately pour the mix into the pan.

Baking

5. Bake the pancake in the lower third of the preheated oven at 428 °F (220 °C) top/bottom heat for about **15–18 minutes**, until the batter puffs up well and the edges turn golden brown. Remove the pan from the oven (the pancake will deflate slightly). Serve immediately, topped with the berries and dusted with powdered sugar.

Makes 4 Servings | Wheat Starter

CARAMELIZED KAISERSCHMARREN

Kaiserchmarren—a true classic from Alpine cuisine and one of the most famous Austrian desserts.

TOTAL TIME
1.5 hours

PREPARATION TIME
30 minutes

RESTING TIME
1 hour

FOR THE SOAKING MIXTURE (OPTIONAL)
40 g raisins
2 Tbsp. rum or apple juice

FOR THE DOUGH
4 medium eggs
60 g sugar
10 g bourbon vanilla sugar
250 g wheat starter
250 g whole milk
1 pinch salt

ADDITIONAL ITEMS
40 g butter for frying
4 tsp. sugar
Powdered sugar for dusting

> **TIP**
> Instead of wheat starter, Lievito Madre starter can also be used.
> In that case, mix 190 g Lievito Madre starter and 310 g whole milk (instead of 250 g in the batter) thoroughly, and then mix it into the whipped egg yolks.

1. For the soaking mixture, mix the raisins and rum. Cover the raisins and let them soak for at least **1 hour**. (They can also be soaked the day before.)

2. For the dough, separate the eggs. Beat the egg yolks with the sugar and bourbon vanilla sugar in a bowl until light and creamy. Briefly stir in the wheat starter and whole milk.

3. Beat the egg whites with the salt in a clean, grease-free bowl using a hand mixer or stand mixer until stiff peaks form. Carefully fold the egg whites into the batter. Then drain the raisins and fold them into the batter.

4. Heat a large pan and melt 20 g of butter in it. Fry half of the batter to make Kaiserschmarren: pour the batter into the pan so that it's about 1 cm thick. Reduce the heat and fry the batter on one side for about **5 minutes** until golden brown. Quarter the batter, flip it over, and fry the other side until golden brown. Then divide the Kaiserschmarren into bite-size pieces, sprinkle with 2 tsp. of sugar and let it caramelize briefly. Keep the finished Kaiserschmarren warm on preheated plates in the oven at 176 °F (80 °C) top/bottom heat. Prepare the second half of the batter in the same way.

5. Dust the Kaiserschmarren with powdered sugar and serve. They pair well with plum compote, fruit compote, or applesauce.

Makes 4 Servings | Wheat Starter

BAKED BANANAS WITH HONEY

Here, banana pieces are fried in batter and served with honey, similar to what you might find in Asian restaurants.

TOTAL TIME
20 minutes

PREPARATION TIME
20 minutes

FOR THE DOUGH
200 g wheat starter
4 tsp. powdered sugar
4 tsp. rice flour
½ tsp. baking powder (optional)
1 pinch salt

ADDITIONAL ITEMS
High-temperature neutral vegetable oil or coconut oil for frying
4 large bananas
4 Tbsp. liquid honey

1. For the batter, briefly mix the wheat starter with powdered sugar, rice flour, optional baking powder, and salt until a thick batter forms.

2. Heat oil in a deep fryer or small pot to about 338 °F (170 °C).

3. Peel the bananas and slice them into pieces about 1 ½ inch (4 cm) thick. Fry the banana pieces in small batches—not too many at once—by dipping each piece individually into the batter, immediately placing it in the hot oil, and frying for about **2 minutes** until golden brown, turning occasionally. After frying, briefly drain the banana pieces on paper towels.

4. Then drizzle the bananas with honey and serve immediately.

Makes 8 Waffles | Wheat Starter

LIÉGE WAFFLES

A recipe for fluffy, thick, and at the same time crisp waffles made from yeast dough. The characteristic feature is the addition of pearl sugar, which caramelizes during baking.

TOTAL TIME	PREPARATION TIME	FERMENTATION TIME
3.5–6 hours	30 minutes	2–4 hours (sourdough) + 1–1.5 hours (dough)

FOR THE WHEAT-MILK SOURDOUGH
50 g wheat starter
50 g warm whole milk (104°F [40°C])
50 g Type-550 wheat flour

FOR THE MAIN DOUGH
Mature wheat-milk sourdough
3 g fresh yeast
2 medium eggs
30 g sugar
10 g bourbon vanilla sugar
175 g Type-550 wheat flour
125 g soft butter
¼ tsp. salt
80 g Belgian sugar crystals (alternatively granulated sugar)

ADDITIONAL ITEMS
Clarified butter for frying

> **TIP**
> Instead of the wheat-milk starter, Lievito Madre can also be used for the batter. Add 120 g refreshed Lievito Madre and 30 g whole milk to the dough.

1. Dissolve the sourdough starter in the whole milk and then mix thoroughly with the wheat flour. Let the dough rise while covered for **2–4 hours** at 86 °F (30 °C) until it has doubled in size.

2. For the main dough, mix all ingredients except for the butter, salt, and sugar crystals, preferably using the kneading hooks of a hand mixer or the flat beater of a stand mixer, for about **5 minutes**, until you have a smooth and soft dough. Then stir in the soft butter and salt. Finally, gently fold in the sugar crystals.

3. Let the dough rise covered at room temperature for about **1–1.5 hours**, until visibly risen.

4. Preheat a Belgian waffle iron and bake the waffles in batches: first, lightly grease the waffle iron with clarified butter. Using an ice cream scoop, place one portion of dough in the center of the waffle iron. Close the lid and bake the waffle until golden brown, which takes about **3–5 minutes**, during which the sugar crystals caramelize.

5. Serve the finished waffles immediately while still warm. Fresh fruit, compote, cream, or vanilla ice cream are wonderful as side dishes.

ABOUT THE AUTHOR

Sonja Bauer is an author, food blogger, and baking course instructor. She lives with her twins and husband in Berlin and has been working in nutrition consulting for many years. As a nutrition expert, she knows exactly what matters when it comes to recipe development. In 2016, she founded her successful food blog "Cookie und Co" and discovered her passion for food photography, bread baking, and sourdough.

She shares her love of baking and cooking online at *www.cookieundco.de*.

ABOUT THE PHOTOGRAPHER

After completing her training as a photographer in a renowned Stuttgart advertising studio, **Julia Hildebrand** pursued a degree in photographic design at the Munich University of Applied Sciences. Since 2010, she has worked as a freelance photographer for editorial offices, publishers, and advertising clients in the fields of food and still life photography. Together with her colleague Ingolf Hatz, she won the 2016 Gourmand World Cookbook Award for "81.6 kg – Food Art Book" and the 2020 Gourmand World Cookbook Award and GAD Silver Medal for "Loretta kocht echt italienisch." *www.augustundjuli.de*

SOURDOUGH INDEX

Rye Sourdough
Asian-Style Crackers 130
Brookies 166
Chocolate-Cherry Cheesecake with Crumble 168
Country Loaf 100
Granola 172
Muesli Bars 176
Onion Tart 80
Porridge Spelt Bread 94
Pumpkin and Cheese Crackers 122
Quick Sourdough Waffles 54
Refreshing Bread for Sourdough Leftovers 90
Rustic Beer Crust 96
Smoky Almond and Bacon Twisted Rolls 106
Spelt and Oat Rolls 114
Spelt Pasta 46
Torta di Nocciole 162
Wholemeal Rye and Spelt Bread 102

Wheat Sourdough
Baked Bananas with Honey 186
Breadsticks with Parmesan Crust 120
Chocolate-Cherry Cheesecake with Crumble 168
Crispy Crackers 128
Crispy Pan Pizza 70
Fermented Apple Pie 154
Focaccia 60
Fudgy Brownies 160
Grandma's Apple Pancakes 180
Herb Crêpes 48
Hobak Buchimgae with Sesame Dipping Sauce 56
Liège Waffles 188
Mediterranean Tomato Galette 86
Overnight Baked Oatmeal 174
Pancakes 178
Plum Cake with Crumble 138
Porridge Spelt Bread 94
Quiche Lorraine 84
Quick Sourdough Waffles 54
Raspberry White Chocolate Muffins 186
Refreshing Bread for Sourdough 90
Semmelknödel 50
Smoky Almond and Bacon Twisted Rolls 106
Sourdough Babka 144
Spätzle 42
Tarte Flambée 78
Wheat Rolls 112
Wheat Tortillas 38
Yeast Braid with Milk Sourdough 148

Lievito Madre
Banana Bread 156
Alsatian-Style Beer Cream Flatbread 76
Blueberry-Quark Cookies 140
Buchteln 152
Caramelized Kaiserschmarren 184
Dutch Baby 182
Fresh Pasta 44
Grissini 126
Italian Pizza 66
Kiymali Pide 72
Naan Bread 36
Olive Oil Brioche Burger Buns 108
Palatinate-Style Steamed Dumplings 52
Pinsa Romana 64
Porridge Spelt Bread 94
Potato Gnocchi 40
Quick Sourdough Waffles 54
Refreshing Bread for Sourdough Leftovers 90
Salmon-spinach Tart 82
Smoky Almond and Bacon Twisted Rolls 106
Swedish Cinnamon Rolls 134
Sweet Rolls 152
Taralli Pugliesi 124
Torta di Mandorle 164

INDEX

Note: Page numbers in *italics* indicate recipe photos.

Alsatian-Style Beer Cream Flatbread, *75*, 76–77
apples
 Fermented Apple Pie, 154–55
 Grandma's Apple Pancakes, 180–*81*
Asian-Style Crackers, 130–*31*

babka, sourdough, 144–47, *145*
bacon
 Alsatian-Style Beer Cream Flatbread, *75*, 76–77
 Onion Tart, 80–*81*
 Quiche Lorraine, 84–*85*
 Smoky Almond and Bacon Twisted Rolls, *105*, 106–7
baking guidelines and tools, 30–31, 33
Banana Bread, 156–*57*
bananas baked with honey, 186–*87*
berries
 Blueberry Quark Cookies, 140–43, *141*

Dutch Baby, 182–*83*
Overnight Baked Oatmeal, 174–*75*
Raspberry White Chocolate Muffins, 158–*59*
Blueberry Quark Cookies, 140–43, *141*
bread and rolls, 89–116
 about: baking guidelines, 30–31; bulk fermentation, 30, 31; guide to recipes, 32; preparing dough, 30; shaping, 30
 Breadsticks With Parmesan Crust, *117*, 120–21
 Country Loaf, *99*, 100–101
 Olive Oil Brioche Burger Buns, 108–*10*
 Porridge Spelt Bread, *93*, 94–95
 Refreshing Bread for Sourdough Leftovers, 90–92
 Rustic Beer Crust, 96–*98*
 Smoky Almond and Bacon Twisted Rolls, *105*, 106–7

Spelt and Oat Rolls, 114–*16*
Wheat Rolls, *111*, 112–13
Wholemeal Rye and Spelt Bread, 102–*4*
breakfast sweets. *See* sweets for breakfast...
Brookies, 166–*67*
brownies, fudgy, 160–*61*
Buchteln (Sweet Rolls), *151*, 152–53

Caramelized Kaiserschmarren, 184–*85*
cheese. *See also* pizza and such
 Breadsticks With Parmesan Crust, *117*, 120–21
 Chocolate-Cherry Cheesecake with Crumble, 168–*69*
 Pumpkin and Cheese Crackers, 122–*23*
 Quiche Lorraine, 84–*85*
 Tarte Flambée, 78–*79*
cherries, sweets with, 168–*69*; q, 176–77

chocolate
 Brookies, 166–*67*
 Chocolate-Cherry Cheesecake with Crumble, 168–*69*
 Fudgy Brownies, 160–*61*
 Muesli Bars, 176–*77*
 Raspberry White Chocolate Muffins, 158–*59*
 Torta di Nocciole, 162–*63*
cinnamon rolls, Swedish, 134–*36*
conversion charts, 24, 32
cookies. *See* sweet baked goods
Country Loaf, *99*, 100–101
crackers. *See* nibbles
crêpes, herb, 48–49
Crispy Crackers, 128–*29*
Crispy Pan Pizza, *69*, 70–71

dessert. *See* sweet(s) *references*
dipping sauce, sesame, 56–*57*
dumplings, 50–*51*, 52–*53*
Dutch Baby, 182–*83*

SOURDOUGH INDEX | 191

Fermented Apple Pie, 154–55
flatbread. *See also* pizza and such
   Alsatian-Style Beer Cream Flatbread, *75*, 76–77
   Focaccia, 60–*62*
   Kiymali Pide, 72–74
   Naan Bread, 36–*37*
   Wheat Tortillas, 38–*39*
flour, European to US conversion chart, 24
Focaccia, 60–*62*
Fresh Pasta, 44–*45*
Fudgy Brownies, 160–*61*

gnocchi, potato, 40–*41*
Grandma's Apple Pancakes, 180–*81*
Granola, 172–*73*
Grissini, 126–*27*

Herb Crêpes, 48–*49*
Hobak Buchimgae with Sesame Dip Sauce, 56–*57*

Italian Pizza, 66–*68*

Kiymali Pide, 72–74

Liége Waffles, 188–*89*
Lievito Madre sourdough, 25–26. *See also* **Sourdough Index** (page 190)

Mediterranean Tomato Galette, 86–*87*
Muesli Bars, 176–*77*

Naan Bread, 36–*37*
nibbles, 119–30
   Asian-Style Crackers, 130–*31*
   Breadsticks With Parmesan Crust, *117*, 120–21
   Crispy Crackers, 128–*29*
   Grissini, 126–*27*
   Pumpkin and Cheese Crackers, 122–*23*
   Taralli Pugliesi, 124–*25*
nuts and seeds
   Asian-Style Crackers, 130–*31*
   Crispy Crackers, 128–*29*
   Granola, 172–*73*
   Kiymali Pide, 72–74
   Mediterranean Tomato Galette, 86–*87*
   Muesli Bars, 176–*77*
   Olive Oil Brioche Burger Buns, 108–*10*
   Overnight Baked Oatmeal, 174–*75*
   Pumpkin and Cheese Crackers, 122–*23*

Smoky Almond and Bacon Twisted Rolls, *105*, 106–7
Taralli Pugliesi, 124–*25*
Torta di Mandorle, 164–*65*
Torta di Nocciole, 162–*63*
Wholemeal Rye and Spelt Bread, 102–*4*

oats
   Granola, 172–*73*
   Muesli Bars, 176–*77*
   Overnight Baked Oatmeal, 174–*75*
   Spelt and Oat Rolls, 114–*16*
Olive Oil Brioche Burger Buns, 108–*10*
Onion Tart, 80–*81*
Overnight Baked Oatmeal, 174–*75*

Palatinate-Style Steamed Dumplings, 52–*53*
pancakes and waffles
   Grandma's Apple Pancakes, 180–*81*
   Liége Waffles, 188–*89*
   Pancakes, 178–*79*
   Quick Sourdough Waffles, 54–*55*
pasta
   Fresh Pasta, 44–*45*
   Potato Gnocchi, 40–*41*
   Spätzle, 42–*43*
   Spelt Pasta, 46–*47*
Pinsa Romana, *63*, 64–*65*
pizza and such. *See also* flatbread
   Crispy Pan Pizza, *69*, 70–71
   Italian Pizza, 66–*68*
   Kiymali Pide, 72–74
   Mediterranean Tomato Galette, 86–*87*
   Onion Tart, 80–*81*
   Pinsa Romana, *63*, 64–*65*
   Quiche Lorraine, 84–*85*
   Salmon-Spinach Tart, 82–*83*
   Tarte Flambée, 78–*79*
Plum Cake with Crumble, *137*, 138–*39*
Porridge Spelt Bread, *93*, 94–*95*
Potato Gnocchi, 40–*41*
preserving sourdough, 27–29
Pumpkin and Cheese Crackers, 122–*23*

Quiche Lorraine, 84–*85*
Quick Sourdough Waffles, 54–*55*

raisins, in Caramelized Kaiserschmarren, 184–*85*
Raspberry White Chocolate Muffins, 158–*59*

recipes, guidelines and tools, 32, 33
Refreshing Bread for Sourdough Leftovers, 90–92
rolls. *See* bread and rolls
Rustic Beer Crust, 96–98
rye sourdough, 20–21. *See also* **Sourdough Index** (page 190)

Salmon-Spinach Tart, 82–*83*
Semmelknödel (Bread Dumplings), 50–*51*
Sesame Dip Sauce, 56–*57*
side dishes, 35–57. *See also* pasta
   Herb Crêpes, 48–*49*
   Hobak Buchimgae with Sesame Dip Sauce, 56–*57*
   Naan Bread, 36–*37*
   Palatinate-Style Steamed Dumplings, 52–*53*
   Quick Sourdough Waffles, 54–*55*
   Semmelknödel (Bread Dumplings), 50–*51*
   Wheat Tortillas, 38–*39*
snacks. *See* nibbles
sourdough. *See also* **Sourdough Index** (page 190)
   about: cooking and baking cakes with, 12
   basics, science, and history, 10–12
   converting types of, 21, 23–24, 26
   European to US flour conversion chart, 24
   fermentation and, 11
   health appeal of, 11–12
   Lievito Madre, 25–26
   preserving, 27–29
   rye, 20–21
   wheat, 22–24
Sourdough Babka, 144–*47*, *145*
Spätzle, 42–*43*
spelt
   Porridge Spelt Bread, *93*, 94–*95*
   Spelt and Oat Rolls, 114–*16*
   Wholemeal Rye and Spelt Bread, 102–*4*
Spelt Pasta, 46–*47*
spinach, in Salmon-Spinach Tart, 82–*83*
starter
   about, 16–19; additional yeast, 18–19; replacing, 18
   establishing, 13–15
   feeding cycles, 16
   hungry, acetone smell and, 16–17
   managing and working with, 17–19
   step-by-step, 14–15

Swedish Cinnamon Rolls, 134–*36*
sweet baked goods, 133–69
   Banana Bread, 156–*57*
   Blueberry Quark Cookies, 140–*43*, *141*
   Brookies, 166–*67*
   Buchteln (Sweet Rolls), *151*, 152–53
   Chocolate-Cherry Cheesecake with Crumble, 168–*69*
   Fermented Apple Pie, 154–*55*
   Fudgy Brownies, 160–*61*
   Plum Cake with Crumble, *137*, 138–*39*
   Raspberry White Chocolate Muffins, 158–*59*
   Sourdough Babka, 144–*47*, *145*
   Swedish Cinnamon Rolls, 134–*36*
   Torta di Mandorle, 164–*65*
   Torta di Nocciole, 162–*63*
   Yeast Braid with Milk Sourdough, 148–*49*
sweets for breakfast and dessert, 171–89
   Baked Bananas with Honey, 186–*87*
   Caramelized Kaiserschmarren, 184–*85*
   Dutch Baby, 182–*83*
   Grandma's Apple Pancakes, 180–*81*
   Granola, 172–*73*
   Liége Waffles, 188–*89*
   Muesli Bars, 176–*77*
   Overnight Baked Oatmeal, 174–*75*
   Pancakes, 178–*79*

Taralli Pugliesi, 124–*25*
tarts. *See* pizza and such
tomato galette, Mediterranean, 86–*87*
tools for baking, 33
Torta di Mandorle, 164–*65*
Torta di Nocciole, 162–*63*
tortillas, wheat, 38–*39*

waffles. *See* pancakes and waffles
Wheat Rolls, *111*, 112–*13*
wheat sourdough, 22–24. *See also* **Sourdough Index** (page 190)
Wheat Tortillas, 38–*39*
white chocolate raspberry muffins, 158–*59*
Wholemeal Rye and Spelt Bread, 102–*4*

Yeast Braid with Milk Sourdough, 148–*49*

Naan Bread - page 36

Herb Crêpes - page 48

Quick Sourdough Waffles - page 54

Focaccia - page 60

Pinsa Romana - page 64

Alsatian-Style Beer Cream Flatbread - page 76

Onion Tart - page 80